A New England Church

A NEW ENGLAND CHURCH

1730-1834

INA MANSUR

The Bond Wheelwright Company
Publishers · Freeport, Maine

Library of Congress Catalog Card #74-76868
ISBN 0-87027-139-3 hardcover edition
ISBN 0-87027-140-7 softcover edition
Manufactured in the United States of America
First printing: June 1974
Published by the Bond Wheelwright Company
Freeport, Maine 04032

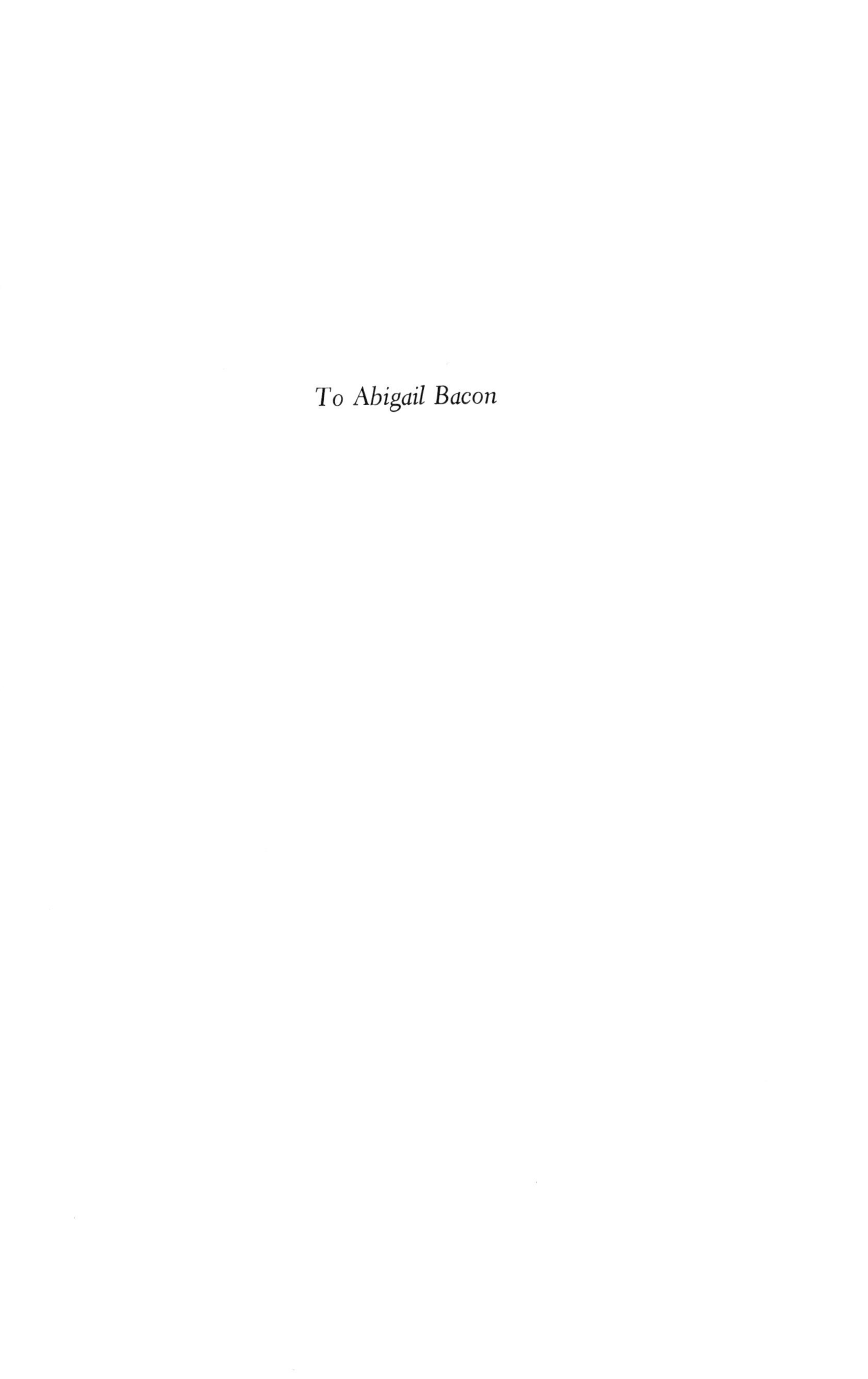

To Abigail Bacon

ACKNOWLEDGMENTS

Without the help and encouragement of many people this book could not have been written. I am grateful to my husband, Lawrence Cutler Mansur, for the preparation of the majority of the illustrations, for his judgment in compiling the references, for his assistance in searching out appropriate material to complete some sections, which were at first meager and thin, and for several critical readings of the whole manuscript. I wish particularly to thank Miss Virginia Wharton who devoted many hours to making the text logical and clear. I am indebted to Mrs. Marcia Moss and Mrs. Barker for their infinite patience in allowing me to work with the reference material in the Concord Free Public Library.

Mr. Norman Fiering kindly read the manuscript and offered invaluable suggestions which I have followed as best I could.

While gathering the information, the librarians in the following places have been understanding and helpful: American Antiquarian Society, Arlington Public Library, Bedford Public Library, Billerica Public Library, Boston Public Library, Connecticut Historical Society, Gardiner Public Library (Maine), Harvard Divinity School, Harvard Public Library, Lexington Public Library, Pilgrim Historical Library, Princeton Library, and the Unitarian Historical Library.

The town clerks in Bedford, Billerica, Concord, and Harvard; members of the Historical Society of East Windsor, Connecticut, and of the Concord Antiquarian Society have been equally helpful.

To all these and more I am grateful.

Ina Mansur

Bedford, 1973

CONTENTS

❧ LIST OF ILLUSTRATIONS ❧

❧ PREFACE ☙

Collecting the material for this book has been like making a journey into a place one can never fully understand. It is about people who lived at another time in another environment for other purposes. They were farmers who left behind them, here on earth, their houses, their children, and their land. Their children were similar to, but not like, them; and their grandchildren were even more diverse.

I am a New Englander who knew little of the path my people had trod, either as Englishmen or as Americans, to reach the twentieth century.

The inhabitants of the town of my childhood were homogeneous. They had a profound sense of freedom; they placed high value on sound education; and they lived a deep faith in a logical sequence of nature. They believed each day would bring a reasonable unfolding of the life of the individual.

One small, white clapboard church had been built near the center of the town, close by the combination town hall and grammar school. It always looked freshly painted and completely closed. I can remember the building being opened only twice. Once parents met there in December and, trying to keep a fire burning, trimmed a Christmas tree. Late that afternoon they gave a party for all the children in the town, complete with candy and popcorn balls, and a gift for every child. Again, on a warm August day, after the hay had been gathered, the church was open one Sunday morning and a lady minister held a service. Everyone came. There was congregational singing. The adults seemed to know the tunes and the words of the hymns. My mother brought the lady minister home with us and gave her a good, freshly cooked meal. I remember asking my parents why the lady did not stay and keep the tiny building open. They said it would not be as wholly good as I, a child, might think.

Now, I believe my parents were the last descendants of people who remembered the travail of the years during which the local churches had split into sects or denominations. They sensed the heartache and the bitterness that was behind them. They had found a way to live in peace with their fellow townsmen; they would not reopen the old wounds.

I was an adult when criticism of the Puritans and their ethics broke across the land. Who were these Puritans, I asked, these straightlaced, narrow-visioned ancestors? I did not know. So I began to read.

Those planters of New England whom I could touch through old books and records seemed a fairly decent lot. Many were well educated and well-to-do. They came to Massachusetts Bay because they had a vision of what they believed would be a perfect life. They spent their strength and their wealth laying the foundations for it. They insisted that people who did not share their dream were to settle in other areas; they wanted a chance to work at making their vision a reality.

The communities they created were surprisingly peaceful. The inhabitants supported a church and a school. They took care of the resident poor and ill among them. They settled misunderstandings and injustices among themselves through compromise, as they said, for peace sake, or to ease their minds about it.

The Reverend Mr. Edward Bulkeley, second minister of Concord (1660–1696), seems to have expressed the attitude of the inhabitants of his town when he asked in a Thanksgiving sermon what could the people do to show their gratitude for the benefits they did enjoy? He felt the quandary was real since the world and absolutely everything in it belonged to the Lord, who had created it. It was incongruous to offer to the Lord what was his already, even in thanksgiving. Mr. Bulkeley's answer was that his people should consider themselves and everything around them as reflecting the generous love of God, the Creator, and they should strive to make the reflection a glorification of Him. This, he said, would be most pleasing to God.

The people of Concord showed they were doing this when the title to their land was questioned by the government in London in

1690. They proved, both by way of deeds and of testimony, that not only had they rightfully acquired the land by grant from the regional government in Boston, but also by agreement and sale from the original owners, the Indians.

The residents had been considerate of their fellow townsmen and had managed local matters on a sectional basis. For those living in an outer section to wish to establish themselves as a separate town was a normal development. The smaller the group, the more important each man in it could be.

No bitterness seems to have underlain the separation of the eastern inhabitants of Concord when they broke away and created a town they called Bedford. The new townsmen seem to have been in harmony one with another, and to have lived in a manner to glorify the Lord's creation as Mr. Bulkeley had counseled.

What, then, went wrong?

Many influences were at work, and for one, the people's dream went awry when it was taken away from them by the Reverend George Whitefield in 1740. He wandered through the land, telling the inhabitants they were sinners by inheritance and could only touch the perfection of God through certain prescribed avenues. The purpose of their lives was to reach a stage of individual purity clean enough to be acceptable to God. Thus their eyes were turned inward upon themselves, and for the first time they began to look askance at their neighbors and to feel they must be circumspect with certain of them, for they could be known by the company they kept.

The atmosphere of the New England towns changed and their churches split apart. The purpose of schools was diverted from sound education to sectarianism, where the method of teaching was more important than what was taught. The vision was distorted. What the dream had been could not be remembered, so it was forgotten.

The story which opened from the material I could reach is chronicled here. The events occurred in one small New England town, but they could have happened in many. The days were heavy with soul-searching, and they ended with a burden cast aside. The people became intolerant of intolerance, and they turned once again to a way of life which seemed reasonable and logical to them, a way they could justify in their own minds. This is the story of their struggle.

Bedford, 1972 Ina Mansur

I

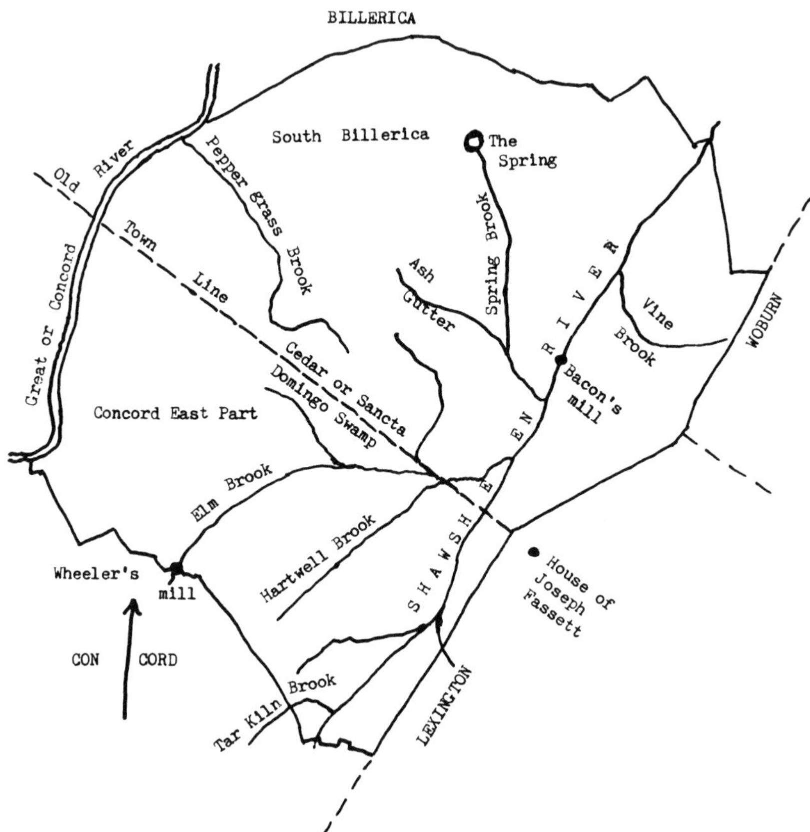

Map 1. South Billerica and Concord's East Part. Compiled from Abram Brown, *op. cit.*, frontis. and p. 101; Charles H. Walcott, *Concord in the Colonial Period, op cit.*; and a map drawn by Stephen Davis, 1760, now in the office of the Bedford town clerk.

THE PLACE, THE PEOPLE, AND THE CHURCH

By the early part of the 18th century, fear of Indian raids was past and the far reaches of the adjacent towns of Billerica and Concord in Massachusetts Bay Province had been nursed into productive farms. Probably twenty families lived in the gentle uplands of South Billerica, the first having come about 1665. Their holdings extended to the town's line with Concord's East Part.

To the south of that line, another twenty families cultivated the deep, black soil of the meadowland. Here there was a tar kiln on one brook, and Wheeler's mill stood on another.

Every other year, on a chosen day in spring, two South Billerica men and two from Concord met at the east end of the town line, at the home of Joseph Fassett in Lexington. (See Map I) From there, they walked into the swamp close by Lexington's line and touched the ax marks on an old pine tree. They tramped northwest, 63½ degrees by today's compass,* reaching the Shawsheen River quickly. The river was wide because it was dammed in South Billerica at Jonathan Bacon's corn and saw mill. Once over the river, the men crossed the northern edge of the meadows where the footing was sure. They could see two or three homes on the meadows. Then they entered Cedar Swamp, which they called Sancta Domingo. Property lines of families in the meadows met in the swamp, for this was their source of firewood. When the four had walked about

---

* Magnetic north was used to lay out boundaries in the 17th and 18th centuries. The variation of magnetic from true north must be considered in correlating old landmarks with modern geological survey maps.

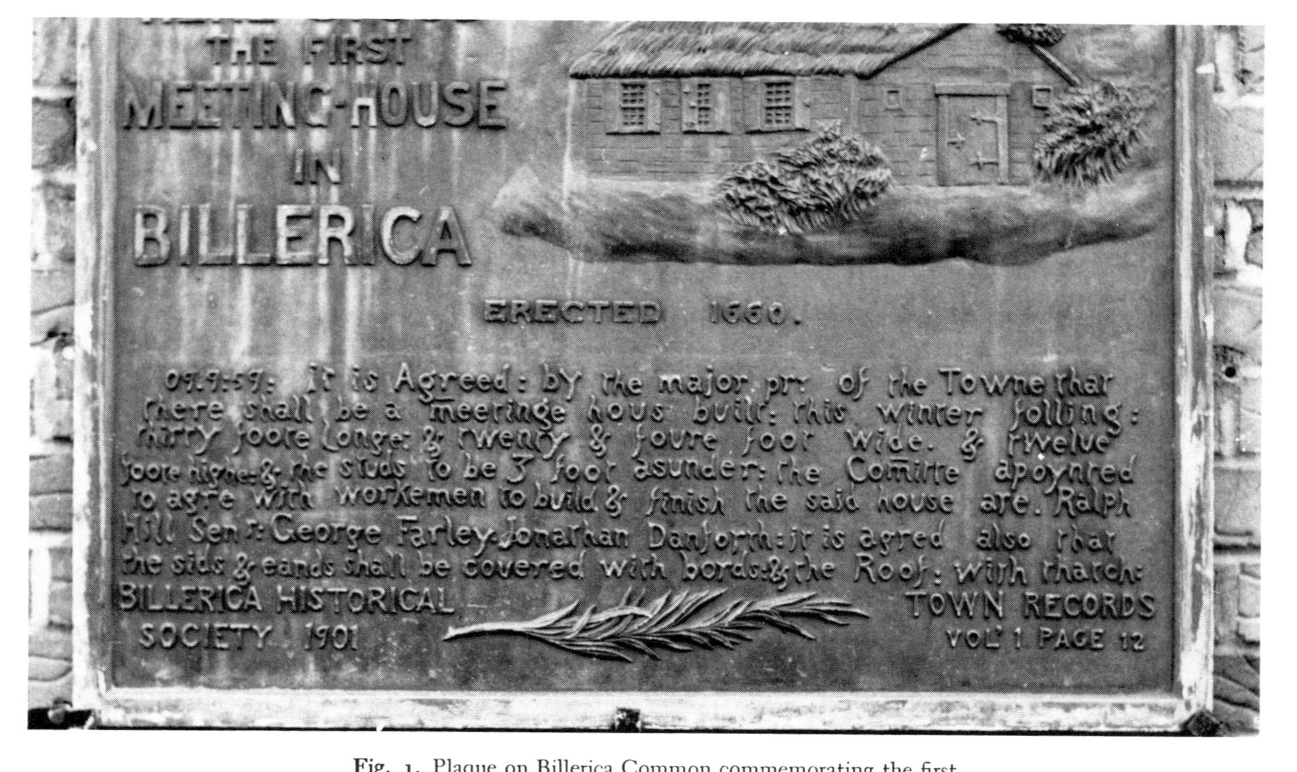

Fig. 1. Plaque on Billerica Common commemorating the first meetinghouse (1972 photograph)

three miles, they came into the flood plain of the Great or Concord River, and they touched the last mark on a tree near the water. They had run the line and made sure that its marks were still clear.

Often the heads of the families traveled to their respective meetinghouses in Billerica and Concord to discuss town affairs with their townsmen. Every Sabbath the families repeated the journey for public worship of God. They had always done this, and they would not neglected their meetings, but every year the ways[1] seemed longer.

The two meetinghouses to which they rode were not alike. In 1725 Billerica's meetinghouse was thirty-two years old, and some could remember the old, thatched roof building it had replaced. (Fig. 1) The townsmen had copied a meetinghouse in edding when they built the second one in 1693. Redding's had been only four years old and it was a new style. An ancient sketch shows it to have been a square building, three windows long, with a hipped roof. The four panels of the roof tapered upward and met over the center of the house at a turret, a belfry, which supported a weathervane. (Fig. 2) Three dormer windows were set into two opposite sides of

Fig. 2. The meetinghouse in Redding which Billerica copied
in 1693

Fig. 3. Concord's third meetinghouse as it was from 1711 to 1790, when it was remodeled (from an old print, *ca* 1775)

the roof to light the galleries inside. There were two doors in the front wall, perhaps one for women and one for men, but the people of Billerica voted to change them to an east and a west door for the inhabitants who traveled from those directions.

Housewrights had assembled sections of the frame on the ground, and many inhabitants could remember the day when everyone gathered to help lift and tie the parts into place or to watch while the work was done. The town's minister, Samuel Whiting, asked God's protection for the men at their work. When the raising was done, the people sang a psalm and gave thanks that no deep harm had come to anyone during the heavy labor.

Although this was the second meetinghouse in Billerica, it was the first style that the Massachusetts Colonists used after they became prosperous enough to abandon clay chinks and thatch. Other examples of this style were the "Old Ship" in Hingham; "Old Lynn," often called the "Tunnel" or "Old Tunnel," in Lynn; and Concord's second meetinghouse.

The families of Concord's East Part shared a large, rectangular meetinghouse, three stories tall, with a gabled roof. (Fig. 3) It was three windows wide and seven long, with a central door in the long side. It stood near the town's millpond, and sheds for tying and sheltering horses had been built at the rear of the house near the pond.

Nothing is known about Concord's first meetinghouse, which had been built probably in 1636. Its second was completed in 1673 with a four-paneled hipped roof like Billerica's. It was used for nearly forty years, but when the third was planned in 1710, the townsmen were asked to choose between the style they had been using, or a second style new to the area. They could have a "bevel" (hipped) roof, or an "English-built."

Concord's people hesitated in their decision for fear of appearing bold and thus exceeding their positions, for they were husbandmen, cordwainers, blacksmiths, and wheelwrights: they were not architects. It was only when they were allowed a written ballot that they felt free to choose the "English-built" by more than two to one.

The people voted repeatedly that the new house would have no turret, nor any place for a bell. The old house near-by was to be used for town and court meetings. It had a bell, and the bellringer could continue his service there.

Half the townsmen gathered on one day, half on the succeeding day, to raise the sections of the building into place. There were thirteen men in the East Part who could have taken their turns at the work.[2] Those residents knew that building from its foundation to the lapped joints of its roof rafters. Soon the knowledge would serve them well.

Although the meetinghouses of the families of South Billerica and Concord's East Part were of different styles, their public worship services were alike. They were in the Congregational Way.[3] There were no other liturgical forms in their towns, nor in towns near-by. There was an Episcopal and a Baptist church in Boston, eighteen miles to the southeast, but they would not have gone there, for they were content.

Their grandfathers had created the Congregational Way soon after they disembarked in New England. This was what they had come to do even while insisting they had not separated from the Church of England by the act of sailing across the Atlantic. It was as though they staked out an area for an experiment in religious and political living and they discouraged persons with dissimiliar dreams from settling there. Their policy could become a model to be copied by all Christian nations, especially by England. They were to build a "city upon a hill." *

The Congregational Way differed from the Church of England in that churchmen were free to select their own ministers and to manage their own church affairs. It was unlike the Presbyterian Church of Scotland, because there was no central control through a hierarchy of ministers or of synods. Each Congregational church was an entity for its own members.

However, there was an examination for membership in any Congregational church. All candidates must have knowledge of religion and all must be holy enough to merit being a member. The first settlers ruled that only churchmen would vote in public matters and hold public offices. Thus they hoped their officials would be good men, administering with insight and justice. In that way there would be no scandal, malfeasance, favoritism, or pressures.

---

* From "A Modell of Christian Charity," written on board the Arrabella by John Winthrop, 1630.

Every town would have its church and the church would be its central influence. A church was created when a group of men signed a covenant, an agreement, to live in a church relationship. Those who signed the founding covenant were the church. Others who attended the worship services were the congregation.

It was hoped that each church would support itself, but only the First Church of Boston was large enough to do this. Members in small towns were too few to pay their ministers' salaries. The Colonial government in Boston decided that all property owners were to be taxed to support the church in their towns. Later all the property in a town would be called a parish and the taxpayers would be members of the parish.

The covenantors promised to keep their church offices filled. They suggested to the townsmen the name of a minister they preferred. The townsmen voted to elect the candidate and they arranged his contract.

The church met in a public meetinghouse which was owned by all taxpayers. Probably there were few towns in the Province with no meetinghouse and where no church was gathered.

In Billerica the gathering of the church was delayed while someone ascertained whether one of the inhabitants, Jonathan Danforth, could have his church membership transferred from Newtowne (now Cambridge) to Billerica. He must be free to sign the organizing covenant and he was not free while he was a member elsewhere. It took five years to get the matter resolved, but at last the church was gathered with him as one of its founders.

The gathering in Concord in 1636 had been unusual. The proposed minister, Peter Bulkeley, lately arrived from England, was residing in Newtowne. The prospective church traveled from Concord to Newtowne to sign the organizing covenant in the presence of Mr. Bulkeley and invited guests. The members returned to Concord, probably to build a meetinghouse and a home for the Bulkeleys. A year later they returned to Newtowne for Mr. Bulkeley's ordination. Only then did the minister, his wife, and their youngest children move to Concord.

It is not known how many inhabitants of South Billerica and Concord's East Part were members of their churches and how many were in the congregations. It is clear that several were devout. More-

over they were members of a neighborhood, even in the presence of
the town line. Young people fell in love across the boundary; families
traded land and moved back and forth; two owned land on both sides
of the line.

Most of the heads of families were third generation descendants
of original planters in Billerica and Concord. Two men were tran-
sients or possible land speculators. One was an absentee owner of
land. Two were bridegrooms who had moved into the area to establish homestead farms. Three men had married into the old families
and, as sons-in-law, were living close to their wives' ties. All were
living about five miles from their meetinghouses.

Soon their religious interests drew them together and they hired
a minister to preach among them instead of continuing their treks
to the meetinghouse.[4] The experiment was successful; they gained
trust and confidence in one another.

Then they drew up and signed petitions which they sent to Billerica and Concord, asking to be set off from those towns so that
they could be united into a township of their own. They owned all
the land they were asking for and the new town lines would be no
problem, since Lexington and Woburn were established on the east,
Billerica on the north, and Concord on the west and south. A petition was received in Billerica as early as 1726, and it was denied.
Its wording has been lost, but the voters in Billerica agreed that the
separation would be damaging and disadvantageous to the town for
several reasons, and they elected a delegate to look after the affair
at the General Court in their behalf.

The petition to Concord has been copied by historians:[5]

> To the gentlemen the selectmen, and other inhabitants,
> of Concord in lawful meeting assembled; the petition of sundry
> of the inhabitants of the northeasterly part of the town of
> Concord humbly sheweth.
>
> That we your humble petitioners, having, in conjunction
> with the southerly part of Billerica, not without good advice,
> and we hope upon religious principles, assembled in the winter
> past and supported the preaching of the gospel among us,
> cheerfully paying in the mean time our proportion to the min-
> istry in our towns, have very unanimously agreed to address
> our respective towns to dismiss us, and set us off to be a distinct

township or district, if the Great and General Court or Assembly shall favor such our constitution.

We therefore the subscribers hereinto, and your humble petitioners, do firstly apply to you to lead us and set us forward in so good a work, which we trust may be much for the glory of Christ and the spiritual benefit of ourselves and our posterity. Our distance from your place of public worship is so great that we labor under insupportable difficulties in attending constantly there as we desired to do. In the extreme difficult seasons of heat and cold we were ready to say of the Sabbath, Behold what a weariness is it. The extraordinary expenses we are at in transporting and refreshing ourselves and families on the Sabbath has added to our burdens. This we have endured from year to year with as much patience as the nature of the case could bear; but our increasing numbers now seem to plead an exemption; and as it is in your power, so we hope it will be in your grace to relieve us.

Gentlemen, if our seeking to draw off proceed from any disaffection to our present Rev. Pastor, or the Christian Society with whom we have taken such sweet counsel together, and walked unto the house of God in company, then hear us not this day. But we greatly desire, if God please, to be eased of our burdens on the Sabbath, the travel and fatigue thereof, that the word of God may be nigh to us, near to our homes, and in our hearts, that we and our little ones may serve the Lord. We hope that God, who stirred up the spirit of Cyrus to set forward temple work, has stirred us up to ask, and will stir you up to grant, the prayer of our petition; so shall your humble petitioners even pray, as in duty bound, etc.

We humbly desire our limits may be extended from Mr. Stephen Davis's to Mr. Richard Wheeler's and to the river, the line to extend so as to include those two families.

The petition was signed by:

Joseph Bacon	John Fassett	David Taylor
Daniel Cheever	Jonathan French	Andrew Watkins
Benjamin Colburn	Joseph French	James Wheeler
Daniel Davis	Nathaniel Merriam	Richard Wheeler
Stephen Davis	Samuel Merriam	Thomas Woolley
Joseph Dean	Zachariah Stearns	

Customarily, services on Sabbaths were held both in the morning and in the afternoon. The luncheon period was two hours. Probably the petitioners were taking their midday meals in local taverns.

On June 3, 1728, the voters of Concord agreed to grant the request of their easterly townsmen. The men of Billerica were still opposed. The petitioners from both settlements had also appealed to the Great and General Court for permission to form a township. Although deputies from Billerica were at the court in Boston to oppose the request, the delegates passed an Act of Incorporation on September 23, 1729, for the town of Bedford, a name the inhabitants themselves had suggested. This was the name of the county in England from which Concord's first minister, Peter Bulkeley, had emigrated in 1635.

The Court made a stipulation: ". . . provided that the said town of Bedford do, within a space of three years from the publication of this act, erect, build, and finish a suitable house for the public worship of God, and procure and settle a learned orthodox minister of good conversation; and make provision for his comfortable and honorable support . . ." [6]

The inhabitants of Bedford had work to do.

II

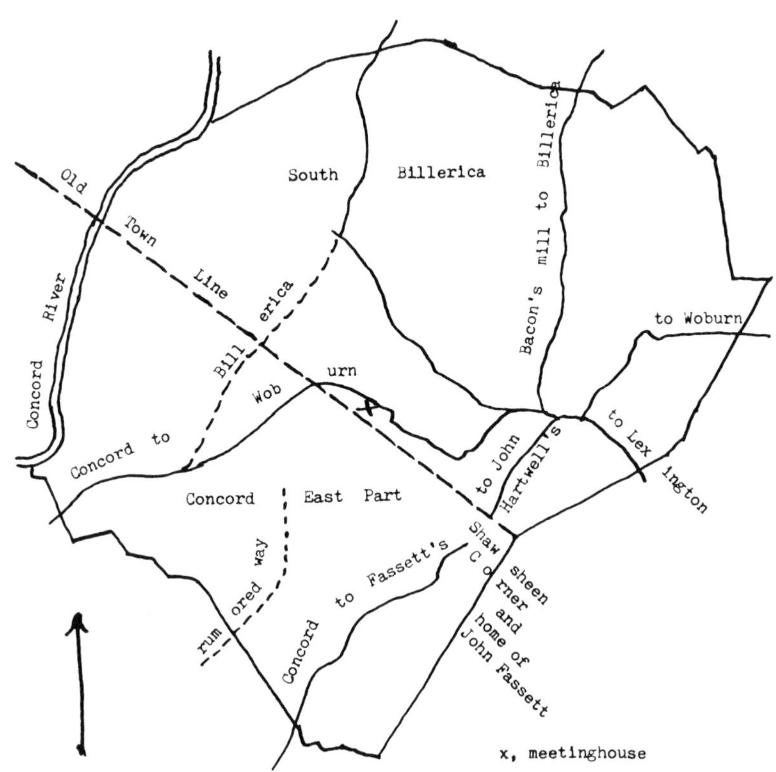

Map.2. Roads in South Billerica and Concord's East Part.
Compiled from Abram Brown, *op. cit.*, frontis.; Billerica town
records, and Concord town records.

✑ THE REVEREND MR. NICHOLAS BOWES ✑

The men of Bedford did not wait for word of the Act of Incorporation before they planned their meetinghouse. They may have met
shortly after they were dismissed from Concord, in 1728, to discuss
its site. The area of Bedford would be a crude circle about three
miles in diameter; it was thinly settled in all sectors. The men wanted
the meetinghouse near the center of the township[1] so that the dis-
tances of travel would not favor one family or small group over
another.

They decided on a parcel of gentle upland overlooking the meadows whose southern boundary was the old Billerica-Concord line.[2]
A road, which they called the road from Concord to Woburn, was
a natural northern line and would save the cost of laying a highway
to the lot. (See Map 2)

They named a committee, men who served until the town was
incorporated sixteen or seventeen months later, to see to the location
and construction of the meetinghouse on this parcel. The committee
bought the land, a nine-acre piece, from Andrew Watkins. It lay
361 feet along the road and extended 1056 feet to the old town line.
An older resident, Joseph Dean, ". . . for and in consideration of the
love of goodwill and affection which I have and bear unto my friends
and neighbors, inhabitants and proprietors in the town of Bedford
. . . to encourage the settling of the gospel among us . . ."[3] gave the
town, through the committee, two strips of three acres each on
either side of the nine acres. Others offered land and the committee
bought some for other purposes, but the meetinghouse was set near

Fig. 4. The first town seal of Bedford

the road on the fifteen acres. Traditionally the land is said to have been wooded, but there is no confirmation.

The committee left no plan of the meetinghouse, nor a record of its style or dimensions. Later, it was remembered as of the second style, gabled. They let the contract for its construction to Joseph Fitch of South Billerica and Richard Wheeler of Concord's East Part for £460.

The exterior of the building was almost complete in the fall of 1729, when the first meeting was called to organize the town. The townsmen voted that the money for the house was to come from a "meetinghouse reat" (rate, tax) levied on all the taxable inhabitants and collected by the two elected constables (tax collectors), one living north of the old town line and one south of it. Joseph Fitch reported that the house had cost more than £460, and he asked for a reevaluation of the contract. The townsmen granted an additional £25, which did not suffice. Richard Wheeler supported Joseph's claim, and was reluctantly granted £75, increasing the total cost to £560.

Four sketches of the meetinghouse are known. Two are on old maps, one is on the town's first seal, and one is a part of the frontis-piece of *History of the Town of Bedford* by Abram English Brown, privately printed in Bedford in 1891. The maps,* drawn by Stephen Davis in 1760 and by Thompson Bacon in 1793, show that a meet-inghouse stood in the center of the town, south of the road to Lex-ington. The seal reproduced the end of a house standing among the stumps of trees, having a V-roof, a central door with a window on either side, and a second story. (Fig. 4) The drawing in the frontis-piece of the *History of Bedford* is of a building five windows long, two stories tall, with a V-roof and no turret. (Fig. 5)

The Reverend Mr. William Stearns, son of the fourth minister to preach in the meetinghouse, described the building in an address given in Bedford in 1868. "The first meetinghouse," he said, "stood on the north side of the Common, very near the road . . . . It had no bell, steeple, tower, or cupola. The underpinning was constructed mostly of small stones, some of which boys would easily remove when they were playing 'hide and seek,' and crawl under it. There were three outer doors, one opening south, one towards the east, and

---

* The maps are in the office of the town clerk.

one towards the west. At each door there was a horse block, designed for the special accommodation of ladies, who often rode to church on a pillion behind their husbands or fathers." [4]

Town meetings were being held in the meetinghouse every two weeks, for it was the only building the people owned, and there was much to plan in a community that had few roads and no school. There was preaching even though the people had not gathered themselves into their church. The townsmen named committees to keep the pulpit supplied with a preacher every Sabbath and to seek a suitable candidate for residency. They found a promising young man sooner than they expected, a Mr. Nicholas Bowes.

All the South Billerica men knew Mr. Bowes because in 1725, at the end of his four-year course of study at Harvard College, he had taught school in Billerica for one term. Then he had returned to the college where, with help from the Hopkins Foundation, he studied debating and public speaking. He was planning a ministerial career and had applied in vain for the pulpit in Dorchester.

Through Nicholas's friendships at Harvard, he had come to know the family of the minister in Lexington, the Reverend Mr. John Hancock. Ties like these he needed, for his own parents were dead. He had an older brother, William, and a younger sister, Dorcas. His parents had been respected people, but not of the ministerial class. His father, for whom he was named, had been a captain at

Fig. 5. Bedford's first meetinghouse, 1730-1816

sea and later had kept a shop on Union Street in Boston. His mother, Dorcas Champney, was from a devout family and the grand-daughter of the elder of Cambridge Church, Richard Champney. William was learning to be a merchant while Nicholas studied for the ministry.

Nicholas had been baptized in Cambridge on November 4, 1706. He had spent many years in school, first in Cambridge grammar school and then in college. (Fig. 6) His curricula included Greek, Latin, Hebrew, logic, philosophy and natural philosophy, divinity, physics and metaphysics, geography, arithmetic, geometry, and astronomy. And now oratory. He had a sound education, but his friendship with Ebenezer Hancock, of Lexington, was almost as important to his career as his training.[5]

Probably Nicholas visited the Hancock home where he met all the family. The older daughter, Elizabeth, and Jonathan Bowman, a student at Harvard, were planning on marriage, since Jonathan had won the pulpit in Dorchester for which Nicholas had applied. One

courtesy Concord (Mass.) Antiquarian Society

Fig. 6. Nicholas Bowes, His Standish

son, Thomas, was starting a business in Boston, as was William Bowes. Another son, John, was a librarian at the college.

Nicholas was attracted to the younger daughter, Lucy, and soon they were making plans to marry when he should be settled in a pulpit and could support a wife. The call from the adjoining town of Bedford was opportune.

The people of Bedford, having a likely candidate, called their first all-day fast to seek guidance in choosing a minister. They invited John Hancock and the ministers of Billerica and Concord, Samuel Ruggles and John Whiting, to conduct the fast-day services. Inside the meetinghouse the atmosphere was subdued, for the humble people wished to be led by the wisdom and will of God and not rely on their own personal choice. The morning service opened with prayer, followed by a reading from the Bible, a psalm, a sermon, a short prayer, another psalm and a blessing. During the recess no one ate food. The afternoon service was similar to that of the morning, and at some time the people voted for a particular candidate. When the service was over, they broke the fast. Within two weeks the name of Nicholas Bowes was sent to a town meeting for concurrence, since all of the voters would be taxed for his salary.

The townsmen offered Mr. Bowes £90 the first year with an annual increase of £1 until he reached a maximum of £100 per year. They offered him, for his encouragement, sixteen acres of land on which they set the value at £9 an acre, and £100 as a settlement fee. (A sixty-acre farm with buildings was worth £256, a cow, £1, and a horse or ox, £2.)

Nicholas did not wish to work for ten years to reach the maximum salary, and he knew the bills of credit, one kind of money in use, were unstable, buying less every year. He wanted an annual supply of firewood for his own hearth, a customary part of ministerial salaries in every town. He proposed to Bedford that he earn £95 the first year, £100 annually thereafter, value to be rated by sterling, and that he be granted twenty-five cords of wood a year.

His reply caused discussion and recalculation, for no townsman wished to be a loser in a financial transaction. They knew twenty-five cords of wood were worth £6 or £7; the salary was another £5. So they needed to justify the expenditure of £11 or £12. But they found a way to do it; they voted to set the value of the land at £8 an acre, a saving of £16. It was the same land they had offered at £9 an acre.

Mr. Bowes assumed his duties on June 1, 1730. On July 13, he wrote a statement of contract in the town clerk's book:

I accept of the encouragement and salary which the town has offered and proposed to me as witness my hand.*

Nicholas Bowes.—

He was ordained on Wednesday the fifteenth, and the church was gathered on the same day. The ministers, deacons, and messengers from the churches in Cambridge, Lexington, Billerica, and Concord were invited to comprise the council to witness the gathering. The ministers from these churches conducted the ordination, and the townsmen granted £15 for entertainment of the guests. This may have been spent at Benjamin Danforth's inn on the Shawsheen River for midday food for the men and their horses.

The ordination was a public ceremony. Nathaniel Appleton, of Cambridge Church, opened the service with a prayer. Probably the people sang a psalm and then John Hancock climbed to the high pulpit to preach from II Cor. 11:28. "Beside those things that are without, that which cometh upon me daily, the care of all the churches." He used similar texts many times, since he was a popular speaker at ordinations, even as he was a peacemaker and moderator. He was a recognized leader among the clerics in the area. He dressed in a powdered wig which fell to the shoulders of his cloak, a white collar, and a pleated white muslin cravat. The wig, cloak, collar, and cravat were the vesture of Congregational ministers. When he had given the sermon, he turned to Nicholas Bowes and charged him with the care of the church in Bedford.

John Whiting extended his hand in fellowship to Mr. Bowes. This symbolic rite had been practiced since the first church had been gathered in Salem in 1629. It welcomed Mr. Bowes to the ministry in the name of all the churches. Mr. Whiting had worked in Concord since 1711, when the third meetinghouse had been built. The men of the East Part had referred to him when they had written ". . . if our seeking to draw off proceeded from any disaffection to our present Rev. Pastor . . . then hear us not today . . ." **

---

* Nicholas Bowes's signature as traced from the town clerk's record book in Bedford.
** From the Petition to Concord.

Samuel Ruggles closed the service with prayer. He had come to Billerica twenty-two years before as Samuel Whiting's assistant and now he had full care of the church.

After the midday recess, the people met to gather the church. The covenant of the church had been made ready, probably by Nicholas Bowes and John Hancock, for the founders to sign. During the previous winter those planning for the church had agreed that "every person admitted to the church should give in a confession of their faith to be read in public,"[6] but no vote was to be taken on the applicants. The founders would have made confessions (or professions) at some time.

The covenant was more elaborate than the simple one signed in Salem a hundred years earlier. Those settlers had pledged: "We Covenant with the Lord and one with another; and doe bynd ourselves in the presence of God, to walke together in all his waies, according as he is pleased to reveale himself unto us in his Blessed word of truth."[7] Bedford's covenant was a Christian and a sectarian agreement, following the tenet of the Covenant of Grace.

THE FOUNDING COVENANT

We, whose names are underwritten, sensibly acknowledging our unworthiness of such a favor and unfitness for such a business, yet apprehending ourselves to be called of God in a way of church communion, and to seek the settlement of all the gospel institutions among us, do therefore, in order thereto and for the better promotion thereof as much as in us lies, knowing how prone we are to backslide, abjuring all confidence in ourselves, and relying on the Lord Jesus Christ alone for help, covenant as follows.

We believe the Scriptures of the Old and New Testament to be given by inspiration of God, and promise by the help of the Divine Spirit, to govern ourselves both as to faith and practice according to that perfect rule; and we also engage to walk together as a church of Christ, according to all those holy rules of the gospel respecting a particular church of Christ, so far as God hath or shall reveal his mind to us in that respect.

We do likewise acknowledge our posterity to be included which we professedly acknowledge ourselves devoted to the fear and service of the only true God, our Supreme Lord, and the

Lord Jesus Christ, the High Priest, Prophet, and King of his church, unto whose conduct we submit ourselves, on whom alone we wait and hope for grace and glory, to whom we bind ourselves in an everlasting covenant never to be broken.

We likewise give ourselves up one to another in the Lord, resolving by his help to treat each the other as fellow members of one body in brotherly love and holy watchfulness over one another for mutual edification; and to subject ourselves to all the holy administrations, appointed by him who is the Head of his church, dispensed according to the rules of the gospel, and to give our constant attendance on all the public ordinances of Christ's institution, walking orderly as becomes saints.

We do likewise acknowledge our posterity to be included with us in the gospel covenant; and, blessing God for such a favor, do promise to bring them up in the nurture and admonition of the Lord with the greatest care, and to acknowledge them in the covenant relation, according to the rules of the gospel.

Furthermore we promise to be careful to our uttermost to procure the settlement and continuance of all the offices and officers appointed by Christ, the chief Shepherd for his church's edification, and accordingly do our duty faithfully for their maintenance and encouragement, and to carry it toward them as becometh us.

Finally we acknowledge and do promise to preserve communion with the faithful churches of Christ for the giving and receiving mutual council and assistance in all cases wherein it shall be needful.

Now the good Lord be merciful unto us, and, as he hath put it into our hearts thus to devote ourselves to him, let him pity and pardon our frailties, humble us out of all carnal confidence, and keep it forever upon our hearts to himself and to one another for his praise, and our eternal comfort, for Christ's sake, to whom be glory forever Amen.[8] ह्ஒ

Churchmen for three generations, at least around Concord, had understood and lived by the Covenant of Grace. Peter Bulkeley had explained it to his church and congregation with such clarity that they had asked him to write it in a book. It was published in London in 1646 as *The Gospel Covenant or the Covenant of Grace Opened.* The Covenant of Grace stated that God loved His people infinitely, and through His great love and generous care He promised to protect and keep each person who followed His guidance and believed in His son, Jesus Christ. It was an agreement never to be rescinded by God. It was open to everyone, except perhaps for the Turks and Papists. Those not accepting it were uncared for and living in sin. God cared for His people here on earth, day by day, and there was a promise, though not a certainty, of life after death. Christ was the mediator who appealed to God in behalf of His people. The covenant was administered through the ordinances of baptism and the Lord's supper. This agreement between God and man was the Covenant of Grace.

One entered into the agreement by learning about it at public worship services, studying it in the Bible and other writings, developing faith in it and in Christ, praying to be accepted, and leading a saintly life such as God would approve.[9] God might touch one through metaphysical means so that one knew, perhaps instantly, that one had been accepted. This was the experience one related when one applied for church membership. Each of the founders of the church in Bedford had had such an experience.

Including the children assured the continuance of the church into the following generations. As children, they had been baptized, and upon growing up and marrying, they would be allowed to have their children baptized without the necessity of relating religious experiences. This custom had been followed since 1662, and Peter Bulkeley had supported it even earlier when he said the covenant in which parents lived applied to their children forever because it was eternal. The practice was called the Half-Way Covenant, since the rite of baptism had been observed but the relation necessary for full membership in the church and for sharing the Lord's supper had not been fulfilled.[10] The day would come when the church in Bedford would question the worthiness of young people to carry on the church without professing their faith and observing communion, but in 1730 no one foresaw the problem, and all were content.

That afternoon twenty-three men, from twenty-four to eighty-one years old, led by young Nicholas Bowes, moved down the middle alley of the meetinghouse and paused to sign the covenant of the church. Eleven had lived in South Billerica, eleven in Concord's East Part, and one was a newcomer. They were:

Abbott, Obed, 33
Bowes, Nicholas, 24
Bacon, Jonathan, 58
Cheever, Daniel, 37
Davis, Daniel, 57
Davis, Eleazer, 24
Davis, Stephen, 44
Dinsmore, Thomas, age
    unknown
Fassett, Josiah, 43
Fitch, Samuel, 56
French, Joseph, 81
Hartwell, John, 57

Hartwell, William, 58
Kendall, Jacob, 69
Kidder, Benjamin, 28
Lane, Job, 41
Lane, John, 38
Merriam, Nathaniel, 57
Page, Christopher, 39
Page, Nathanel, 51
Putnam, Israel, 31
Taylor, David, 31
Wheeler, James, 28
Wheeler, Richard, age
    unknown

There were at least twenty-two other men living in Bedford who may have been heads of families.[11] None was a founder of the church, although five became pew owners, one joined the church later, and one sat in the congregation.

Of the forty-six or so families in the town, the Benjamin Kidders, the Israel Putnams, and the Josiah Fassetts lived within walking distance of the meetinghouse. (See Map 3) All the others rode in on horseback, and the townsmen planned to build horsesheds as soon as they could. One was to stand north of the meetinghouse and one to the south.

Inside the building, the gallery was not to be installed until the people had completed the payments for the house. But the pulpit and a block of seats on either side of the middle alley must have been in place, as the house continued to be used. So these furnishings belonged to the townsmen and were provided by Joseph Fitch and Richard Wheeler. Two of the seats have been kept until today, and one has the date "1728" cut into the outside of the back plank.

About two weeks after the gathering on August 4, 1730, the church elected two deacons. They were Israel Putnam, formerly of South Billerica, and Nathaniel Merriam, once of Concord's East Part. These two had three duties: they were to accept gifts and offerings in the name of the church, distribute church funds to the needy, and provide and serve the bread and wine at communion.

Had the church been gathered thirty years earlier, two elders might have been named as well as the deacons. When John Hancock

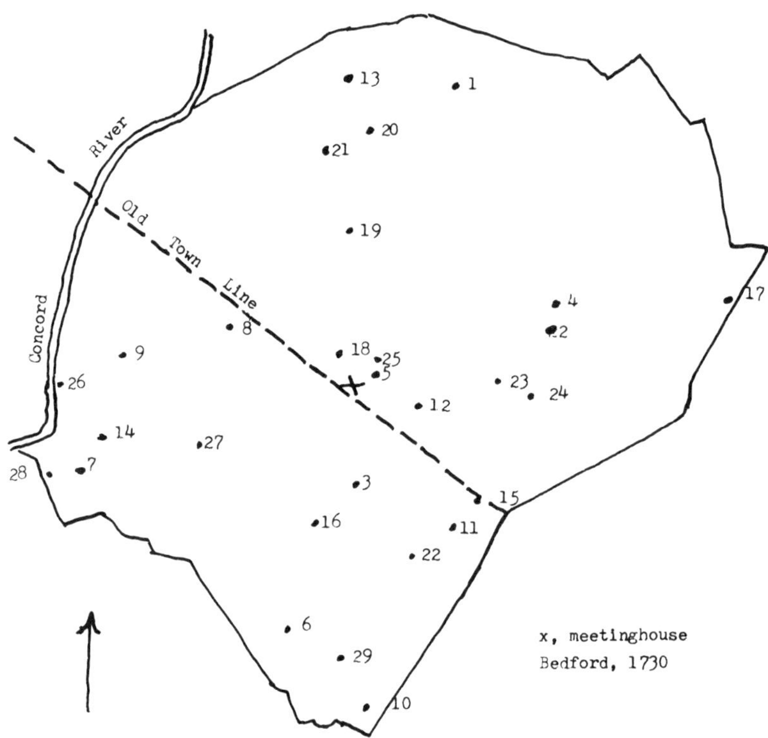

Map 3. Approximate homesites of the covenantors and honorary pew owners in Bedford:

1. Obed Abbott	11. John Fassett	21. John Lane
2. Jonathan Bacon	12. Josiah Fassett	22. Nathaniel Merriam
3. Joseph Bacon	13. Samuel Fitch	23. Nathaniel Page
4. Josiah Bacon	14. Joseph French	24. Christopher Page
5. Nicholas Bowes	15. John Hartwell	25. Israel Putnam
6. Daniel Cheever	16. William Hartwell	26. David Taylor
7. Benjamin Colburn	17. Jacob Kendall	27. James Wheeler
8. Daniel Davis	18. Benjamin Kidder	28. Richard Wheeler
9. Eleazer Davis	19. James Lane	29. Thomas Woolley
10. Stephen Davis	20. Job Lane	

The homesite of Thomas Dinsmore has not been ascertained.*

---

* Compiled from information in Abram Brown, *op. cit.*,
frontis. and *passim*; Bedford records 11/29/1731, 3/8/1734-
35, and 5/19/1735; Billerica records; Concord records; and
Registry of Deeds, North, *op cit.*

first settled in Lexington he was asked if he would like his church to name elders and he replied he would. "The duties of the elders have never heretofore been very well defined . . ." he said, "but latterly they have settled down to this: the younger elder is to brush down, and harness the pastor's horse, when he wishes to ride out, and the elder elder is to accompany the pastor when he goes out of town and pay his expenses. I should like very well to have such officers chosen." [12] Lexington church did not elect elders, nor did Billerica, Concord, and Bedford.

About two months after the gathering, Nicholas Bowes conducted the first communion for the members of his church. After the public worship service, the congregation left the house while the members remained to be served the elements by the deacons. They used temporary flagons and tankards; their table may have been a shelf hinged to the face of the pulpit. Two months later (November 12) at the first all-day thanksgiving, money was given for the deacons to buy a tablecloth, a napkin, a basin, two dishes, two flagons and four pewter tankards.

The church shared communion every other month and observed a fast in spring and an autumn thanksgiving each year. The Provincial government named the days of fast and thanksgiving, but the church was free to call others if the members felt the need.

While the gallery was being built, the townsmen named a committee to "lot out" pew ground on the meetinghouse floor. They marked areas where private pews could be built, each six feet eight inches long and four feet seven inches wide. The people approved this, then at a town meeting, drew up rules for granting pew lots.

    Vote, for the man and his wife to sit in the pue, excepting the deacons

    Vote, there shall be but one poll to an estate in seating the meetinghouse and pues

    Vote, they are to have respect to them that are fifty years of age or upward

    Vote, those that are under fifty years are to be seated in the meetinghouse according to their pay

    Vote, they that have pues, they shall have them according to what they have paid to the meetinghouse

    Vote, the front foreseat in the gallery to be equal with the third below in the body of seats.[13]

A committee was selected to grant the lots, and five men over fifty were seated first:

Deacon Nathaniel Merriam was assigned to the town's pew reserved for deacons on the east side of the pulpit. He had been Concord's banker, handling as much as £50,000 to £60,000 in bills of credit that were issued in Boston annually. Farmers borrowed from this fund each spring and tried to repay with interest in the fall. Mr. Merriam had been in charge of the loans and collections, a responsible duty he had faithfully performed. Probably this was the reason he was named deacon of the Bedford church.

John Fassett had moved from Malden to Billerica with his family when he was about nine years old. He had grown up listening to the sermons of Samuel Whiting and later Samuel Ruggles. Shortly after his marriage with Mary Hill, daughter of Mary Hartwell Hill, he had been given Hartwell land in Shawsheen Corner by his wife's uncle, John Hartwell. He lived on this land in the northeast section of Concord's East Part, so John and Mary went to Concord to hear John Whiting, nephew of the Samuel Whiting John had heard in Billerica. His medical background is not known but his grave was marked with the title: Dr. He chose to sit in the meetinghouse "at the west end, north of the door adjacent to the window." [14]

Daniel Davis was born in Concord. His farm lay on the road from Concord to Billerica, near his nephew Eleazer. He and his wife Mary had raised ten children and probably had helped Eleazer's mother Eunice with her family of seven after the early death of Eleazer's father. Daniel and Mary sat opposite John Fassett at the east end adjoining Josiah Bacon's pew north of the east door.

William Hartwell and his wife Ruth lived on the edge of the meadows. He had not signed the petition to be set off from Concord, but he had given £5 toward the expense of creating a new town. He served on the committee to seek a minister and to seat the meetinghouse. He selected the second pew at the east end of the meetinghouse, against the north wall, a cold place, but one close to the minister and the Bible lessons.

Nathaniel Page had come to South Billerica from England with his family when he was a lad. He and John Fassett shared the same sermons. Nathaniel had married a neighbor's daughter, Susanna Lane. Many years later it was their oldest son, Nathaniel Jr., who carried a banner among their possessions to the opening battle of the Revolutionary War. Even later it was given to the town and is still called the "Bedford Flag." [15] Nathaniel chose to sit in the approximate position he had used in Billerica Meetinghouse, at the front of the building, east of the entrance.

The order of seating those under fifty has been lost, and at least one refused his seat, writing in the town clerk's book:

"I, the subscriber, do in the presence of the selectmen, relinquish pew ground allotted to me by the committee that lotted out the pew ground in the meetinghouse, that lot in the northwest corner of the meetinghouse, as witness my hand, Richard Wheeler." [16]

Richard knew tragedy. His only son died in infancy and his wife was young when she too died. Later he married his neighbor, Widow Eunice (Potter) Davis.

However, eight men under fifty were seated: Joseph and Josiah Bacon; Job, John, and James Lane, Stephen Davis, Thomas Woolley, and Benjamin Colburn.

Joseph Bacon was Deacon Merriam's brother-in-law. He had moved from Billerica to Concord's East Part, where he was the Deacon's neighbor, shortly after his marriage. He chose to sit in the northeast corner of the meetinghouse, adjoining William Hartwell's pew, because William was another neighbor.

Josiah Bacon was a young man with five sons. He and his wife Mary chose a pew at the east end of the meetinghouse adjoining that of his uncle Joseph Bacon.

Job, John, and James Lane, brothers of Susanna (Lane) Page, shared their grandfather's farm. The family was devout. Their grandmother was Hannah Rayner, a minister's daughter. The brothers agreed that no one could create a more perfect home life than daughters of the clergy. Job married Martha Ruggles, sister of the Reverend Samuel Ruggles. John selected Catherine Whiting, daughter of the Reverend Samuel Whiting. Both Martha and Catherine were of Billerica. James chose Martha Minot of Concord, daughter of James, a teacher and a doctor, and sister of Timothy, a teacher and a minister. Because of their interest in clerical matters, the Lanes were to have an unusual influence in the Bedford church.

Job and Martha sat opposite William Hartwell on the north side of the meetinghouse. John and his second wife (Catherine was dead) were on the south side, west of the entrance, adjoining Thomas Woolley's pew. James and Martha had the second pew from the entrance, adjoining that of Nathaniel and Susanna (Lane) Page.

Stephen Davis was Daniel's youngest brother. His pew was separated from Daniel's by a doorway, since he sat at the east end of the meetinghouse, south of the east door, adjoining the women's stairs.

Thomas Woolley's mother and Benjamin Colburn's wife were sisters. Thomas selected the pew in front on the west side, under the second window from the "great door" in the meetinghouse. Benjamin chose the pew lot at the west end of the building, south of the west door, adjoining the men's stairs. Uncle and nephew were on either side of the stairs. (Fig. 7)

Twelve of the thirteen pew owners had held town offices. The exception was William Hartwell who had been elected constable for South Bedford, but had declined to serve. He was uninterested in civil affairs, but devoted to the church and committed to his covenant.

Families related to one another often lived near-by in neighborhoods. The choice of pew lots reflected a similar arrangement: two

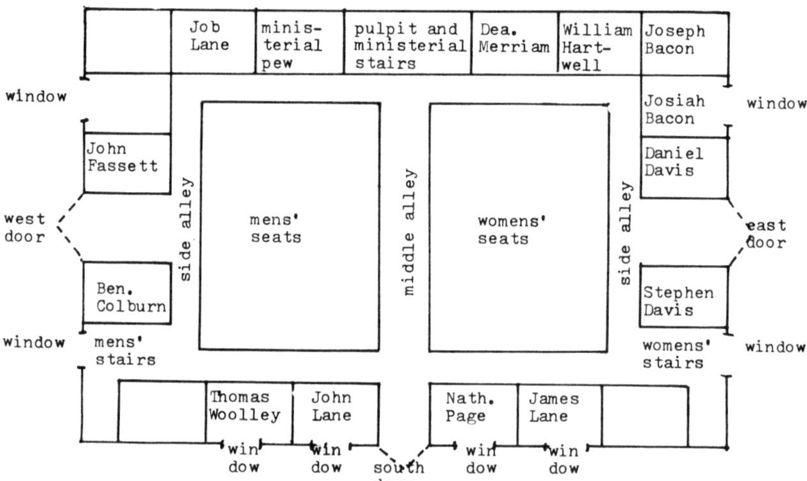

Fig. 7. Seating plan in Bedford meetinghouse, 1734* (drawn from information obtained in Bedford town records)
* Scale: 8 feet to 1 inch

Bacons, two Davises, two Lanes and their sister, and Thomas Woolley and his uncle were neighbors in the meetinghouse.

These thirteen pew lots were the only honorary ones the townsmen ever granted. The lots were areas, nearly square, where each recipient arranged his pew by laying his floor about three inches above the original, placing benches around three sides of the lot, and setting an entrance gate along the fourth, next to the alley. The seats of the benches were hinged so that they could be tipped up for ease in standing, and the tops of the backs were trimmed with railings. Probably each pew seated six or eight persons, and some sat facing away from the pulpit.

There were four vacant lots which may not have been used. The seats on either side of the middle alley were a women's and a men's section, held in common by the town, and left open for the congregation.

When a committee gave Nicholas Bowes the deed to his land, he found it to be in four separate pieces, all near the meetinghouse. Four and a half acres lay south of the land around the house; five, east of it; six, across the road northeast of it; and a half acre, east of the five acres and separated from it by about 370 feet. He decided to build his house on the six-acre piece. (Fig. 8) Perhaps Joseph Fitch built it, since he was completing the meetinghouse, even the gallery.

Nicholas and Lucy Hancock were married by the time their house was finished and in May 1733, the townsmen voted to deliver firewood to Mr. Bowes's house in Bedford. They also said that the pew built next to the pulpit stairs was to be the ministerial pew. Lucy Bowes was seated there, beside Job and Martha Lane, during public worship services, fasts, thanksgivings, and the ordinances her husband conducted.

Now that the honorary pew lots were recorded, four townsmen requested that they be given lots. They were the covenantors Obed Abbott and Josiah Fassett; the land donor, Joseph Dean; and the deacon, Israel Putnam.

Obed hoped they would grant him the pew ground adjoining Thomas Woolley's next to the men's stairs. Obed, a weaver, had brought his bride Elizabeth Tarbell from Salem, to live on a sixty-acre farm north of Bedford's spring. He served in several town offices and was the town treasurer for many years, but he was not allowed to sit beside Thomas Woolley. Probably his meetinghouse

courtesy the Concord Free Public Library

Fig. 8. Home of the Reverend Mr. Nicholas Bowes

rate had been too small. Obed held no rancor; he worshipped in that house for forty years and was the last covenantor to die.

Josiah Fassett wanted a pew beside that of his brother John. Josiah had his father's large farm north and east of the meetinghouse, but he had sold some of it to John Hartwell and indirectly to Israel Putnam. He was denied pew ground, perhaps because he had paid too little toward the building.

Joseph Dean hoped "they would give him his right in the pew ground according to what he had done as others have in the town." He asked for "six foot in length in the two hind seats below on either side of the middle alley." [17] The amount of his meetinghouse tax is not known, but he must have felt the gift of land worth £50 should have been taken into account. He wanted to sit where the town kept seats for the congregation, and he was not permitted to do this. The seats were guarded as an investment and when they were removed, it was for a public, not a private, cause.

Israel Putnam moved from Salem to South Billerica when he married Sarah Bacon, the miller Jonathan's daughter. He owned

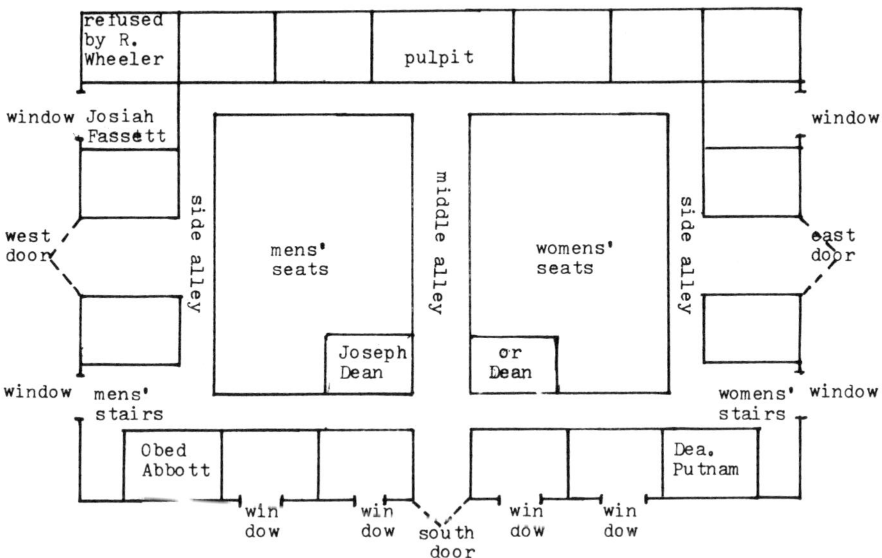

Fig. 9. Requests for pew lots denied, 1733-34* (drawn from information obtained in Bedford town records)
* Scale: 8 feet to 1 inch

Fig. 10. Meetinghouse at Alna, Maine. The rail around the
building is for tying horses (1970 photograph)

one hundred and fifty acres as well as a tavern and a hennery. His home was called a "mansion house." His meetinghouse rate was probably ample for a pew lot. He asked for the ground adjoining Ensign James Lane's pew, which was next to the women's stairs in the meetinghouse. The pew east of the pulpit was kept for the deacons; Israel must have been asking for space for Sarah and their children. Mrs. Merriam was not granted a lot, and Israel did not get one for Sarah. The deacons' wives must have been seated in the women's seats with the congregation. Nevertheless, Israel Putnam was a deacon of Bedford Church for thirty years, until he died.

The requests of these four men were voted on separately and separately denied. They were not discouraged, for when they wrote another petition, they induced Nicholas Bowes to sign with them. This too was unsuccessful. The assignment of any part of the meetinghouse was a civil affair and in such matters the minister had only one vote. (Fig. 9)

When the lots on the floor of Bedford's house are drawn to scale, the area appears to have been about fifty feet long and thirty-four feet wide. The great entrance door was in the middle on the south with two windows on either side of it. A middle alley led from the great door to the pulpit in the middle on the north. Both the east and west doors were flanked by a window on either side. The middle alley separated a block of seats into a women's and a men's section. The pews stood around the perimeter of the floor except at the doors, the stairs, and the pulpit. Side alleys separated the pews from the seats. Stairs to the gallery were at the southeast and southwest corners.

Such a house has been preserved in Alna, Maine. When its floor plan is compared to Bedford's and to that of the first style in Billerica, it is seen that slight modifications in the alleys were made to adapt the floor plan to a small or a large house, using one, two, or three doors. Alna's house seated 500, Bedford's about 350, and Billerica's probably about 350. (Figs 10-14)

Mr. Bowes was administering the ordinance of baptism thirteen or fourteen times each year. The housewright Joseph Fitch and his wife Sarah (Grimes), of Lexington, brought their firstborn child to the meetinghouse for the ordinance. Joseph was baptized the same day, but it is not known whether he related a religious experience and became a full member of the church, or held half-membership.

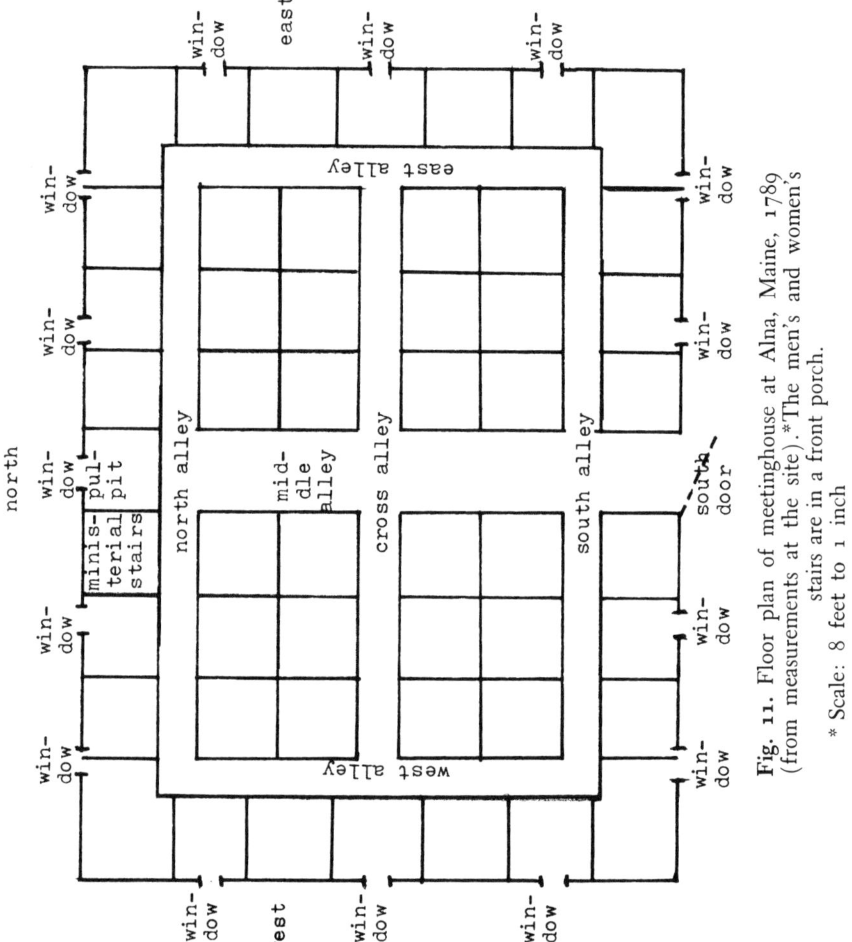

Fig. 11. Floor plan of meetinghouse at Alna, Maine, 1789 (from measurements at the site).*The men's and women's stairs are in a front porch.

* Scale: 8 feet to 1 inch

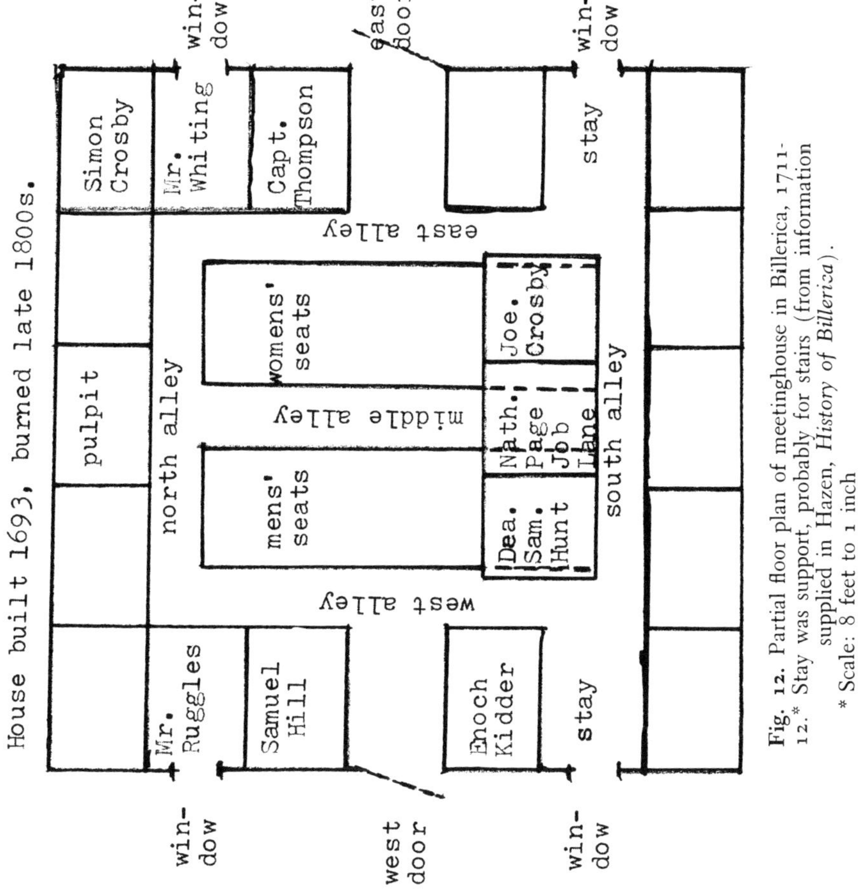

Fig. 12. Partial floor plan of meetinghouse in Billerica, 1711-12.* Stay was support, probably for stairs (from information supplied in Hazen, *History of Billerica*).
* Scale: 8 feet to 1 inch

Fig. 13. The high pulpit on the north wall of the meetinghouse at Alna, Maine (1971 photograph)

Fig. 14. The square pews on the ground and in the gallery,
Alna, Maine (1971 photograph)

Nicholas did not believe the produce from sixteen acres would augment his salary sufficiently to support a family. The Hancocks owned fifty acres. They had raised five children, two of whom were graduates of Harvard College. Before his marriage, Nicholas bought from Josiah Fassett eight acres east of his home lot and from Joseph Dean nine acres which connected his gift of five acres to his half acre. After his marriage, he bought five on the Concord River from Benjamin Colburn, making his holdings thirty-eight acres.

Lucy's brother, Ebenezer Hancock, came to Bedford to teach for a short time, making his home with the Bowes. When Ebenezer was ordained in Lexington in 1734 to assist his father, Nicholas took part in the ceremony.

After the Bowes had been married about a year and a half, their first child was born. He was named William in honor of Nicholas's brother William, of Boston. When he was four days old, he was baptized by his grandfather, even as Nicholas had been baptized during the first week after his birth. Soon Nicholas increased his home lot to ten acres and his farm to forty-two by buying four acres from his neighbor, Deacon Israel Putnam.

Before Lucy Bowes gave birth to her second child, a girl named Lucy, Nicholas purchased three acres from Job Lane. When a third child, a son named Nicholas, came, the father did not add to his farm. Nor did he increase it at the birth of Elizabeth, named for Lucy's sister Elizabeth. However, when the fifth child, named Dorcas for Nicholas's sister, arrived, he bought three and a half acres from Deacon Merriam's brother Samuel. His farm was now nearly fifty acres and it was large enough.

In 1735 Mr. Bowes rode to Burlington with his two deacons for the ordination of the first minister, Supply Clapp. Burlington was a new town, part of Old Woburn, so perhaps the church was gathered the same day and Bedford's messengers were in the council.

Mr. Bowes had served his church eight years when two of the original covenantors died.[18] Early one morning Stephen Davis went to the meadow to scythe by the brook. When he did not return, his family searched for him and found him fallen beside the swaths he had cut. They left him a plain stone to mark that place and wrote these words for his tombstone in the burying place:

Here lyes Buried
ye Body of
Mr STEPHEN DAVIS;
Who Rested *From* his labour
Att his labour, July ye
11th, *Anno Domni* 1738 in ye
53d Year of His Age.

(Fig. 15)

That fall Deacon Nathaniel Merriam died. His mother-in-law, Eunice Taylor, had bequeathed £5 to Bedford Church in the Deacon's honor, and the Deacon too remembered the church. Someone, probably Deacon Putnam, ordered a silver communion cup* from Jacob Hurd of Boston to be inscribed: "The Gift of Dea'n Nath'l Meriam to the Church of Christ in Bedford with a legacy of £5 from E. Taylor, 1738." [19] The Deacon's tombstone was cut in simple dignity:

Here lyes Buried
ye Body of Deacon
NATHANIEL MERIAM:
Who Departed this
life Decbr 11th: 1738. Aged
66 Years & 1 Day.
Ye Memory of ye Just is Blessed.

(Fig. 16)

His position in the church was filled by the devout Job Lane. Both Deacon Lane and Deacon Putnam lived north of the old town line, but Bedford was nine years old and the former boundary was no longer significant. In the meetinghouse, Job moved to the east of the pulpit into the Deacon's pew while Stephen Davis's son had his father's pew.

If Nicholas was saddened by these events, his grief deepened because Ebenezer Hancock passed away at the age of thirty, leaving Lucy's father, who was sixty nine, with the full care of the Lexington church.

---

* See Fig. 47.

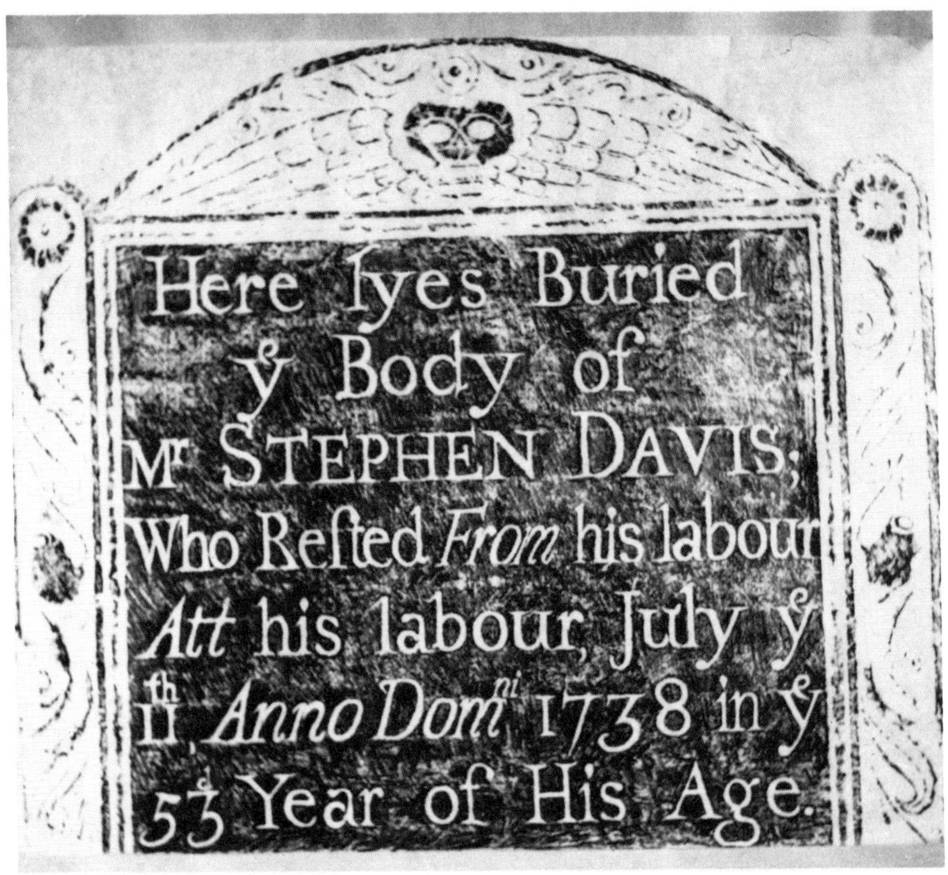

Fig. 15. Stephen Davis's tombstone (from a 1971 rubbing)

Fig. 16. Deacon Nathaniel Merriam's tombstone (from a 1971 rubbing)

The people of Lexington did not replace Ebenezer because they were hard pressed for money. The Province continued to print bills of credit until they had little worth. Nicholas had been wise to protect his salary with the value of silver. The townsmen of Bedford contributed quarterly to supplement his income. In succeeding years they added £20, £30, £40, annually to £100, and finally were adding £320 when England declared it illegal for the Province to issue money and took action to stabilize the currency. Mr. Bowes's salary became £50 13*s* 4*d* lawful money, and his previous currency was called "old tenor."

Mr. Bowes's church continued to grow. Seven new members were admitted to communion and full membership each year in a town of about fifty-six taxable estates. He read the candidates' confession of faith before the church, and they subscribed to the covenant. He encouraged confessions of sin, written statements of penance for intemperance, theft, or a broken commandment. These he read aloud, probably hoping they would be moral lessons for his congregation. He was a man of sound evangelical sentiments, that is, one whose sermons were biblical analogies, one who sought conversion through friendship. He followed the Covenant of Grace, demonstrating it as he presided over the pulpit.

Upon this scene of births and deaths, of land, money, ordinances, confessions, fasts, and thanksgivings burst in 1740 a turmoil. It was small at first, but it was to envelop all of New England Congregationalism for almost a century. It was called the Great Awakening.[20] It started as a frontier revival in the Connecticut River Valley in 1734-35, although there had been preludes. The Reverend Jonathan Edwards of Northampton, Massachusetts, preached a series of revival sermons designed to bring members of his congregation into a state of salvation. They were emotional in content, but Edwards did not deliver them with emotion. As a young man, he had experienced an insight into the nature of God which has been described as his conversion. From that time his philosophy grew but did not change. He believed God was Excellency. A perfectly designed tool was excellent because nothing could replace it. God was supremely excellent for He had made the world for His own joy in such a manner that the portions fitted together systematically in a miraculous way. Anything which enhanced the whole was good, and man was good as soon as he learned to fit into the excellency of the whole. Man's responsibility was to catch a glimpse of the glory of Excellency and to consent to serve in the total divine scheme. Man ought to reflect the emanation of God. Man was sinful if he upset the divine order God had established everywhere.

The experience of insight was instantaneous and could come to anyone. Once blessed, man found justification by testing his new state with activity. If this enhanced the whole, his experience was genuine. Continuing tests led to faith. In this way, God brought about man's conversion; faith did not. Faith resulted from its occurrence and practice.

This philosophy was Calvinistic and reflected Edwards's personal experience. It departed from the Covenant of Grace by rejecting faith as a primary aid to man's salvation and by disregarding any agreement between God and man.

During Edwards's first revival, those who received the insight of salvation through his quiet words were ecstatic. Jonathan's daughter Sarah, a child of seven, experienced something of God's supremacy. Those who saw only their own guilt were in despair. They asked, "What shall I do to be saved?" Jonathan's uncle Joseph became so depressed he killed himself. The excitement lasted about three mouths before life in the valley became less tense and lapsed into a condition usually called normal.

Five years later, excitement came to the Bay area when an orator, a roving minister from England, a man devoting his life to answering the question, "What shall I do to be saved?" came to travel and preach.

He was the Reverend George Whitefield, a graduate of Oxford, and ordained by the Bishop of Gloucester to the ministry of the Church of England. He was a friend of John Wesley, the founder of Methodism, and he agreed with Mr. Wesley on many religious matters: that is, sin abounded in England; man must find a new, spiritual way of life; man could become regenerate through God's intercession; man's inner state of grace could be judged by his outer actions.

However, Wesley believed man was a responsible being; he could learn to love God; he had the native ability to direct himself toward his own improvement; perhaps God would approve his effort and

Fig. 17. The Reverend George Whitefield

help him. This was Arminianism, named for the man who first taught it, Jacob Arminius (1560–1609).

Whitefield disagreed. He believed this doctrine was sinful because God was the only means of man's salvation. Man was descended from Adam and Eve, who had disobeyed God. They had sinned and man continued to live in sin until, or unless, God willed his conversion and salvation and named him one of the Elect. Whitefield was not an original philosopher. John Calvin (1509–1564) had preached the doctrine of election and it had reached into many churches.

Whitefield was on his second trip to America in 1740 when Benjamin Colman, of Boston, invited him to New England to speak. He sailed by sloop from Georgia to Rhode Island and traveled overland toward Boston. He was met by the governor's son and a group of ministers and inhabitants who escorted him into the town. He lived at Mr. Colman's brother-in-law's house and preached in Old South meetinghouse and many other places.

He was a dramatic speaker. His voice was rich and musical; it was so powerful that Benjamin Franklin believed it could be heard by 30,000 people, even outdoors. He gestured, and every motion was meaningful. His magnetism was in his emotional force, in the way he delivered his sermons. He was a master of elocution.

Many of his sermon titles were from biblical material. They could have been the opening words of worship services or the subjects of lessons. The minister of Roxbury said Whitefield's sermons were Puritanism revived.

However, if a person heard a series of Whitefield's sermons, he would have found distortion of the Covenant of Grace by which many provincial churchmen were living. Bulkeley had said God gave the covenant to Abraham, and all of his descendants inherited it. Whitefield said God gave it to Christ. If the Son would offer His soul as a sacrifice for sin, God would give the Elect faith and repentance. The Elect were those whom Christ would choose. They would enjoy eternal life, a source of everlasting happiness. They would "inherit the kingdom prepared for [them] from the beginning of the world."[21]

Whitefield delivered his sermons extemporaneously. The people who heard him found the experience colorful, emotional, and sometimes depressing. The response the sermons evoked was probably one reason why the Archbishop of Canterbury and the Bishop of London had received the itinerant coldly, and the Bishop had asked "whether his journals were not a little tinctured with enthusiasm."[22]

Whitefield made a circuitous journey of one hundred and seventy miles north of Boston, preaching sixteen times, and visiting, among other places, Ipswich and Newbury. (Fig. 17) When he returned to Boston, he gave a farewell sermon and prepared to visit Jonathan Edwards at Northampton.

Twenty thousand people gathered to hear Whitefield's last sermon in Boston, and he preached it out of doors because no meetinghouse was large enough for the crowd. Because of his enthusiasm, some meetinghouses had been denied him in England, and dissension was beginning to rise in New England.

He had criticized Harvard College because "tutors neglect to pray with and examine the hearts of their pupils who read bad books such as the works of Tillotson and Clarke." [23] He had accused the New England clergy of being "teachers of unsavory and unprofitable religion," "men who were in fact unconverted and destitute of vital piety." [24] These comments made many ministers unhappy, but others said his work was effective and answered a need to save souls.

Of the events of October 13, Whitefield wrote: "About noon I reached Concord. Here I preached to some thousands in the open air; and comfortable preaching it was. The hearers were sweetly melted down . . . The minister of the town being, I believe, a true child of God, I chose to stay all night at his house, that we might rejoice together. The Lord was with us. The Spirit of God came upon me, and God gave me to wrestle with him for my friends, especially those then with me. They felt his power. Brother B[lis]s, the minister, broke into a flood of tears, and we had reason to cry out it was good for us to be here . . ." [25]

"Some thousands" gathered to hear Mr. Whitefield, he wrote, but the entire adult population of Concord was scarcely 1,000. People must have ridden in from the surrounding towns just as Nathan Cole did about ten days later when Whitefield had visited with Edwards and was traveling south, down the Connecticut River Valley, toward Philadelphia. Nathan told about it in his journal.

⁝ . . . All on a sudden, about eight or nine o'clock there came a messenger and said Mr. Whitefield . . . is to preach at Middletown this morning at ten o'clock. I was in my field at work. I dropped my tool that I had in my hand and run home and run through my house and bad my wife get ready quick to go and hear Mr. Whitefield . . . and run to my pasture for my horse with all my might, fearing that I should be too late to hear him. I brought my horse home and soon mounted and took my wife up and went forward as fast as I thought the horse could bear it. And when my horse began to be out of breath, I would get down and put my wife on the saddle bad her ride as fast as she could, and not stop or slack for me, except I bad her. And so I would run until I was almost out of breath, and then mount my horse again. And so I did several times to favor my horse. We improved every moment to get along as if we were fleeing for our lives. All the while fearing we should be too late to hear the sermon, for we had twelve miles to ride double in a little more than an hour . . . . And when we came within about half a mile or a mile of the road that comes down from Hartford . . . to Middletown on high land I saw before me a cloud or fog rising, I first thought of from the great river. But as I came nearer the road, I heard a noise, something like a low rumbling thunder. I presently found it was the rumbling of horses' feet coming down the road, and this cloud was a cloud of dust made by the running of horses' feet down the road. It rose some rods into the air over the tops of hills and trees. And when I came within about twenty rods of the road, I could see men and horses slipping along in the cloud like shadows. And when I came near, it was like a steady stream of horses and their riders. Scarcely a horse more than his length behind another, all of a lather, and some with sweat, their breath rolling out of their nostrils in the cloud of dust. Every jump every horse seemed to go with all his might to carry his rider to hear the news from heaven for the saving of their souls. It made me tremble to see the sight, how the world was in a struggle. I found a vacancy between two horses to slip in my horse. And my wife said, "Law, our clothes will be all spoiled. See how they look." For they were so covered with dust that they looked almost all of a color, their coats and hats and shirts and horses . . . . When we got down to the old meeting-house there was a great multitude of people assembled together. We got off from our horses and shook off the dust. And the minister was then coming to the meetinghouse. I turned and looked toward the great river and saw the ferry boats running

swift, forward and backward, bringing over loads of people.
The oars rowed nimble and quick. Everything, men, horses, and
boats, all seemed to be struggling for life . . . . When I saw
Mr. Whitefield come upon the scaffold, he looked almost an-
gelical, a young, slim, slender youth before some thousands of
people, and with a bold undaunted countenance. And me hearing how God was with him everywhere as he came along, it
solemnized my mind and put me in a trembling fear before he
began to preach, for he looked as if he was cloathed with au-
thority from God.

Later Nathan Cole added,

And my hearing him preach gave me a heart wound. By God's
blessing my old foundation was broken up, and I saw that my
righteousness would not save me . . . . And he had decreed
from Eternity who should be saved and who not. I began to
think I was not elected, and that God made some for heaven
and me for hell. And I thought God was not just in so doing.
I thought I did not stand on even ground with others, if, as I
thought, I was made to be damned. My heart then rose against
God exceedingly for his making me for hell. Now this distress
lasted almost two years . . .[26] ८⋙

Nathan Cole rode almost twelve miles to hear Whitefield. It was
only a few miles from Bedford to Concord. The experience for those
who rode was reflected in the life of Bedford Church for almost a
hundred years.

The immediate effect of Whitefield's work was divisiveness. Was
the emotional climate he produced healthy inasmuch as his sudden
conversions brought on bodily contortions, prostrations, weeping,
and uncontrollable excitement? Was this God's work, or the devil's?
Whitefield had censored both the college and the clergy. Censor-
iousness spread to the pews; members of congregations censored their
ministers and their neighbors, wishing to draw away from sinful associates and become a saved society. Some felt they were more
qualified to preach than their ministers, and lay preaching arose.
Others said Whitefield taught doctrinal errors and questioned the
ethics of itinerancy itself. The social relation between people and
clergy, and between people themselves, was interrupted. The clergy
separated into a group called the New Lights, who supported White-

field's work, and a group called Old Lights, who opposed his methods.

In some towns disagreement in the pews resulted in one faction walking away to begin a church of its own in another part of the town. This was the case in Concord. The town was committed to the Reverend Daniel Bliss, twenty-five, "bold, zealous, impassioned, and enthusiastic." [27] He was a New Light. Part of the congregation, the Old Lights, withdrew and met in a local inn called "The Black Horse" after its business sign. Several times the Old Lights appealed to the town for an abatement of their ministerial tax so they could use that money to hire regular preaching at the inn. They were always denied, so they got preaching as they could, sometimes relying on John Whiting, who was retired but living in Concord. They never managed to obtain a full-time minister.

In Billerica Samuel Ruggles had built a community of love and respect during his pastorate of forty-two years, and there was no sign of dissatisfaction in his congregation.

John Hancock of Lexington understood the challenge and conducted public services to give opportunity for enthusiastic persons to become members of his church, but his sermons did not commit him to the revivalists' way. His policy was successful.

Nicholas Bowes had an example to follow in his father-in-law. Bedford Church did not fracture.

On January 1, 1744-45, Mr. Bowes attended a meeting of the Ministers' Association in Cambridge called by Nathaniel Appleton of that church to ask for advice from his colleagues. George Whitefield had landed at York (now in Maine) from England and was traveling toward Boston. He had asked the minister, the church, and the congregation at Cambridge to invite him to speak there. What reply ought Mr. Appleton send him? [28]

John Hancock moderated the meeting. The ministers who attended with Nicholas were William Williams, of Weston; Warham Williams, of Waltham; John Cotton, of Newton; Seth Storer, of Watertown; Ebenezer Turell, of Medford, and Samuel Cooke, of West Cambridge (now Arlington).

Mr. Hancock opened the meeting, supplicating God for guidance. The members discussed the coming visit thoroughly. They considered the conditions still lingering in the towns, and several pleas were made favoring Whitefield's second tour. Then they considered the

" As many as were in debt came to David, and he became a captain over them."

[p. 110.

Fig. 18

objections to his principles, expressions, and conduct, pointing out that he himself had not explained nor given Christian satisfaction for them.

The ministers voted unanimously that Whitefield should not be invited to speak in Cambridge meetinghouse and they agreed no one of them would invite him into their pulpits. Every minister present signed his name to the agreement.

At this meeting Nicholas Bowes took a stand.

A week later the *Boston Evening Post* declared Mr. Bowes's position: "Bowes subscribed to the 'Seasonable Thoughts' of the Old-Light Champion, Charles Chauncy, and publicly declared that he would not admit the revivalist George Whitefield to his pulpit." [29]

Nicholas and Chauncy had shared at least one year at Harvard College together before Chauncy had been ordained in the First Church of Boston. From that pulpit he became a leading opponent of revivalism. He wrote several pamphlets refuting the Great Awakening, point by point, and "Seasonable Thoughts" was one of them. He said the movement aroused animal nature; it was immoral when it appealed to passion; it was wrong when it used terror as a means. Moreover, he believed conversions were possible without shrieking, swooning, and rapture. Reason ought to guide man toward understanding and a renewed life while his emotions were controlled. It was a statement of the Old Light position, and Mr. Bowes agreed with it.

During the winter of 1744–45, Whitefield lived in Boston where he became involved with the military expedition against the French at Louisburg, Cape Breton. The governor invited Colonel William Pepperrell to lead the attack.

The Colonel and Whitefield were friends, and Whitefield gave Pepperrell a motto for his flag, *"nil desperandum, Christo Duce."* Enlistments had been lagging, but under the religious banner men crowded to volunteer. Two who joined were John Lane of Bedford and Jonathan Hoar of Concord.

The Colonel asked Whitefield to go as chaplain, but the minister said he was preaching three times a day, and thought that more important. Among other places, he preached in Chelsea and Malden.

Samuel Moody, of York, was named chaplain in his place. Whitefield preached when their sailing was imminent and again in thanks-

Fig. 19. Tombstone of Thomas Bowes (1970 photograph)

giving when word of the surrender of Louisburg reached Boston. When the troops returned, it was learned that Joseph Moody, son of Samuel, had held a day of fast at York for the success of the assault, and it happened to be the very day Louisburg fell.

Prior to the second visit of Whitefield, Lucy Bowes lost her oldest brother, John. He had had the pulpit in Braintree and had been another voice of the Old Lights, now not heard. Lucy had only one remaining brother, Thomas, in her family.

When Lucy's third son was born, he was named Thomas for her brother, and the fourth daughter was Lydia, named after Thomas's wife Lydia (Henchman) Hancock. Three weeks before little Thomas's third birthday he died. It was in May, the season when the family would have been planting the garden, and everyone said he choked on a bean. Perhaps it was a hard, shiny seed-bean. Nicholas and Lucy prepared a headstone for his grave, a small one because he was a little boy. They had it trimmed with a border of stylized leaves, and they carefully planned the inscription to be cut beneath a winged mask of death:

> Here lyes Buried ye
> Body of THOMAS
> BOWES, Son of ye
> Revd. Mr. NICHOLAS &
> Mrs. LUCY BOWES;
> Who Died. May ye
> 21st: 1750. Aged 2
> Years 11 Monts & 3 Ds

They laid the body in the burying place and on the gravestone they counted the days he had lived.

Two years later, Lucy's father, John Hancock, died. He was nearly eighty-two and he had preached in the meetinghouse in Lexington as long as he lived. Nathaniel Appleton wrote a memorial biography in Mr. Hancock's honor, praising his judgment, leadership, and talent as a moderator in times of strife. He believed the public life of Lexington reflected Mr. Hancock's personality; with another guide it would have become a different kind of town.[30]

Mr. Appleton may have had in mind the lesson in arbitration Mr. Hancock had taught when he heard two inhabitants quarreling over the position of their boundary. He stood near the limits of the properties, listening to their arguments. At last he drove a stake into the ground, and speaking to both proprietors, he said the stake would make the bound for as long as they agreed it should.

Moreover, Mr. Appleton may have believed the inhabitants would have split into two congregations without John Hancock, as those in Concord had. Division probably was a source of irritation in civic life. Mr. Appleton felt that the people of Lexington had learned from Mr. Hancock's diplomacy how to settle differences.

On March 5, 1753, the inhabitants of Bedford met to celebrate the twenty-fifth year after their first meeting in 1728. They considered this to be their anniversary rather than the date of the incorporation of the town or the date of the completion of the meetinghouse. They decided upon a common act for the common good in observance, the purchase of a bell.

To raise the money, they voted to sell eight pew lots in the meetinghouse, the area occupied by the two hind seats on both sides of the middle alley.[31] The lots were to go to people who had no assigned seats, but no one could buy more than one. Ironically, this included the pew ground which Joseph Dean had wanted twenty years earlier. Now he was dead and would not be bidding.

The sale was an auction in a form called a "vendue." The vendue master auctioned positions on a list of choices. The highest bidder had first choice among the eight lots to be sold. The second highest had his choice among seven. The lowest got the one remaining lot.

Stephen Hartwell, son of the founding William, bid £74 and chose the foremost pew lot on the women's side of the middle alley, a space like the pews against the walls. One of William's other sons must have inherited his pew.

Hugh Maxwell selected for £72 the foremost pew lot in the men's side next to the middle alley. This was like Stephen's. Hugh had fled from persecution in Ireland and had settled on a farm near Jonathan Bacon's mill in 1731. His son Hugh said his parents taught him as a child the principles of freedom and religion which supported him through many hardships.

For £63, Lieutenant Joseph Fitch had the foremost pew lot on the men's side next to the west door. It was seven feet long and four feet seven inches wide. Joseph, now a widower, had built the meeting-house and had served in an armed force, perhaps at Louisburg.

John Bacon paid £66 for fourth choice and chose the foremost pew on the women's side next to the east door, a space like Joseph's. John and his wife, a Billerica woman, worshipped in Bedford's church and used the town's burying place, but it is believed they lived in Billerica. Earlier, inhabitants of one town did not worship in another. John's case may have been the first instance of freedom of choice.

John's brother Benjamin bought the hindmost pew lot on the women's side next to the middle alley for £58. Benjamin was a religious man who had married into the devout Lane family, selecting Colonel John's daughter Catherine.

Sixth choice went to Jonathan Woolley for £55, for the hindmost pew lot on the men's side next to the middle alley. It was six feet in length and four feet seven inches in width. Jonathan was a brother of the convenantor, Thomas. He never married, but he owned a pew.

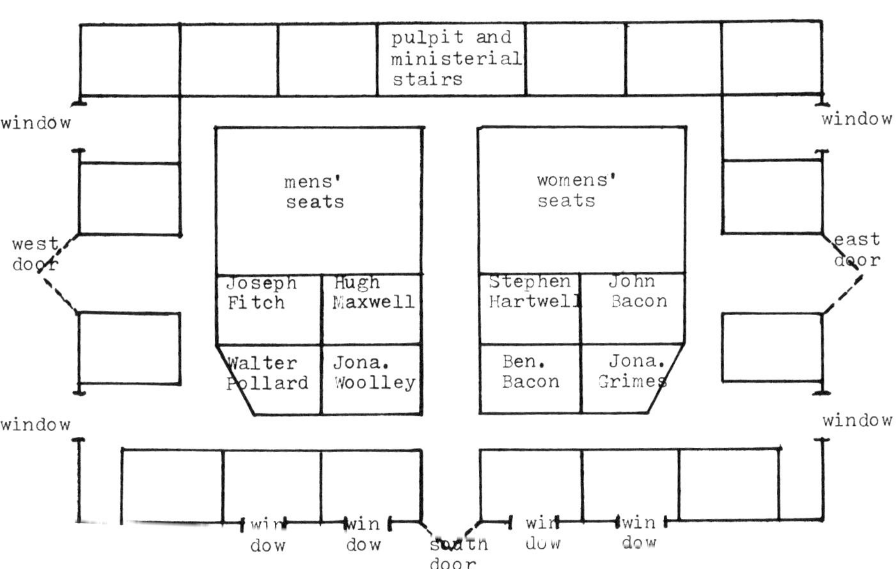

Fig. 20. Sale of pew ground * to buy a bell, 1753 (drawn from information in Bedford town records)
* Scale: 8 feet to 1 inch

Walter Pollard paid £45, buying the hindmost pew lot on the men's side next to the stairs. It was seven feet long in front, four feet eight inches long in back, four feet seven inches wide, and beveled at the end next to the alley. Walter had moved from Billerica soon after 1730, keeping an inn near the center of the town.

Joseph Fitch's brother-in-law, Jonathan Grimes, paid £35 for the remaining choice, the hindmost on the women's side, next to the stairs. It too was beveled next to the alley. Jonathan and his wife had little use of it, for they moved to Amherst, New Hampshire, shortly after he bought it.

The people sold no more ground than was necessary for the purchase of a bell and the cost of hanging it. (Fig. 20) They obtained £468 from the sale. They voted to hang the bell in a tower which they set two and a half rods north of the schoolhouse, as close to Benjamin Kidder's wall as they could "with conveniency." This was not near the meetinghouse, for Kidder's land did not abut the land around the house.

At the twenty-fifth anniversary celebration, many original founders were gone and the second generation was replacing them.[32] The public demeanor of the younger men was cooperative, helpful, and unemotional. Yet there was an inner tension, for a fateful quarrel had begun with Nicholas Bowes before the bell tower was completed.

The immediate or specific cause of the eruption is not known. Nicholas Bowes was an Old Light who agreed with John Hancock and Charles Chauncy. Old Light ministers constructed their sermons carefully and usually read them from small notebooks so that the reasoning of the discourse was kept in order. They expected their congregation to learn the value of loving God and walking well, an idea developed in the Covenant of Grace. A community of people believing in this pattern was adhesive; the inhabitants clung together, respecting both one another and the officials they chose to govern them.

In a town whose minister was a New Light, the sermons were presented extemporaneously, with emotion, eloquence, and enthusiasm. The services were theatrical in a province where there was but little theater. The minister expected instantaneous conversions frequently, and his church was a society of saints proud of their sainthood. A group of saints in an unconverted society tended to be critical of members of that society and disrespectful to governing representatives. In an extreme case, a person believed God was indwelling and he must follow the inner light regardless of society's laws. This attitude was called Antinomianism.

The social tension arising from these two positions caused everyone to evaluate himself and to align with what was right for him. So in Connecticut, people regrouped into denominations of Anglicans, Presbyterians, Baptists, Quakers, and Congregationalists. In Northampton, Edwards cast aside the Half-Way Covenant and, having no halfway membership, insisted on a church of saints. In Concord, the New Lights controlled the town's church until Daniel Bliss died in 1764.

In Bedford, the church became angry at Nicholas Bowes. It has been written that he did "indiscreet acts." John Hancock was no longer alive for advice and consolation. It seems possible that the church asked Mr. Bowes to teach the necessity of instantaneous conversion, and that he refused, saying it was not a necessity, and that he himself had had no such experience but rather had worked day by day at his own salvation. Then the church would have considered him an Arminian, a "teacher of unsavory and unprofitable religion," a man "unconverted and destitute of vital piety." [33]

Nathan Cole, of Connecticut, had been an Arminian before he rode as fast as his horse could bear to hear the Reverend George Whitefield. "When I was young," he wrote, "I had very early convictions; but after I grew up I was an Arminian until I was near thirty year of age; I intended to be saved by my own works such as prayers and good deeds." [34] This may also have described Nicholas Bowes; confessing it would have been "indiscreet."

What did happen was that immediately after the public thanksgiving service of November 1, 1753, the town paid Stephen Minot, of Concord, for preaching in the Bedford meetinghouse. Apparently the break was abrupt, and soon it became final.

Stephen Minot, a nephew of Mrs. James Lane, was twenty-one, a recent graduate of Harvard College. His father Timothy was a member of Daniel Bliss's New Light church. He also was trained for the ministry and substituted in nearby vacant pulpits.

Either the church in Bedford refused to allow Mr. Bowes to preach, or Mr. Bowes would not preach for a church which accused him; however, he was appointed to teach school for five months that winter. The cause of his rejection could not have been based on morals, as parents trusted him to teach their children. He must have been accused of an ecclesiastical error.

The church heard both Stephen and his father Timothy. Stephen was traveling a circuit of vacant pulpits with two other young men, all of whom were available for ministerial contracts. One was Aaron Putnam, of Reading, Deacon Israel Putnam's nephew. John Hancock's pulpit was offered to him, but he refused, saying he wanted to settle in a pioneer town. He went to Pomfret, Connecticut, a community where his distant relative, the famous General Israel Putnam, had settled about fourteen years before. Aaron lived all his days in Pomfret. He developed into a strong Calvinist and as an old man wrote a paper explaining his reasons for believing Universalism to be wrong.

Aaron preached in Bedford and so did the third young man, Jonas Clark, of Newton. He, too, was invited to fill Lexington's pulpit, and he accepted. He continued Hancock's work with the justice and good sense it had enjoyed.

Benjamin Adams, thirty-five, of Newbury, came to preach once or twice. He had been twenty-one when Whitefield spoke in Newbury. Soon he was to be settled in the pulpit in the second parish in Lynnfield.

Each of these men preached only one or two Sabbaths, and the town depended upon Josiah Stearns, of Billerica, who came for six weeks. He was a recent graduate of Harvard College who was teaching in Billerica and living at home where his family had lived for a hundred years.

The supplies for the pulpit* cost £25, or six months' salary for one minister. The pulpit was not vacant and it could not be offered to any of them. The friction between the church and Mr. Bowes was not a topic of business at town meetings. No committees were named to keep the pulpit filled. The situation was tense and secretive; it should have been brought before a council of neighboring churches for discussion and advice. This was not done.

Instead, the church held a regular meeting on August 22, 1754, to act on the matter. To create a semblance of justice, an out-of-

---

* The "supplies" were men preaching as interim ministers so that there would be no loss in divine teachings.

town person was invited to conduct the meeting. Someone asked Jonathan Woolley, now living on the western edge of Bedford, to ride west from his home to Littleton with a message. It is believed he was to invite the Reverend Daniel Rogers of that town to be the moderator in Bedford meetinghouse. The town paid Mr. Woolley for the errand.

Daniel Rogers, the man chosen moderator, apparently understood the New Light movement. He was the son of Dr. Daniel Rogers, and his wife Sarah, of Ipswich, and a member of a large family of ministers, some of whom were Whitefield's friends.[35] In fact, two of his cousins had caused a broil in a meetinghouse in 1742.

When this arrangement for the meeting was complete, Mr. Bowes knew he was defeated. He wrote his resignation. As soon as the meeting opened, he presented it.

> To the Church of Christ in Bedford,
> Brethren,
> Under the present situation of affairs in this town I apprehend that my usefulness as a minister is at an end among you. Therefore I desire that you would give me a dismission and that the relation between me and you as pastor and people shall entirely cease.
>
> Nicholas Bowes

The church voted to comply with Mr. Bowes's request. There was one further piece of business for the meeting.

> Upon Mr. Bowes' offering to the church satisfaction for whatever had been amiss in his conduct among them, it was voted that he be owned and treated as a brother in good standing in charity.[36]

Daniel Rogers signed the report of the church meeting in the town clerk's book, and Nicholas Bowes, Deacon Israel Putnam, Deacon Job Lane, and Stephen Davis signed the agreement of dismissal from the church.

Eleven days later, the townsmen voted to concur with the church in dismissing Mr. Bowes. Thus the Reverend Mr. Bowes became the first of four resident ministers to be dismissed by the town of Bedford in its first hundred years.

As senior church deacon, Israel Putnam was named moderator for the town meeting wherein the contract between his neighbor and minister and the town was terminated.

With the pulpit vacant, townsmen elected a committee, including Jonathan Woolley, to keep it supplied. During the next two years many churchmen served on that committee, and at times the tension was so high that they were selected by secret ballot. Preaching went on in the meetinghouse.

Benjamin Adams returned for one Sabbath. A Mr. Holyoke, probably Eliezur Holyoke who was to have Boxford's pulpit, preached twice. Joseph Perry, who took the Second Church in South Windsor, Connecticut, spoke four times. And Josiah Stearns came for five months, holding eight days of fast for the church, or more than one a month. The fasts indicate the church was disturbed, probably wondering if it had been too unfair. The church may have offered the pulpit to Josiah, but he said he had not decided to give up teaching for the ministry.

The pulpit seems to have been vacant in the spring.

Lucy Bowes gave birth to her eighth child and fourth daughter that winter, a girl they named Mary. There were no known ancestors in the parents' families whose name the infant bore. She was simply Mary Bowes.

Mary's father was now a schoolteacher. However, he was to find a way to reenter the ministry. He soon became a chaplain to the army in the French and Indian Wars.

The Canadian French traders had built a fort at Crown Point on the southern end of Lake Champlain. It was a threat to English and Dutch settlements in western Massachusetts and the Hudson River Valley. Three thousand five hundred provincials were sent there to push the French to the north. They built Fort Edward as a supply base on the Hudson. Material was carried from Fort Edward to Fort Anne and Fort William Henry, both on the waters of Lake Champlain.

A regiment from Middlesex (county) led by the Louisburg veteran, Colonel Jonathan Hoar, was preparing to leave Concord for Fort Edward. Captain Stephen Hosmer, of Concord, had one of the Colonel's companies. Stephen's father was a member of the Black Horse Church, the group that did not conform to the teachings of the New Light enthusiast, Daniel Bliss.

Nicholas Bowes, now forty-nine, enlisted as chaplain in Captain Hosmer's company. Space was set aside at Fort Edward for the observance of public worship services, fasts, and thanksgivings. This was the place where Mr. Bowes was to preach.

The company left Concord in mid-September, 1775. There were two routes west, the northern being the more direct. It led through Marlborough, Worcester, Ware, Belchertown, and Hadley, where there was a ferry across the Connecticut River. West of the river the route ran through woods much of the way, turning northerly to Hatfield and westerly to East Windsor, William's Fort in Pittsfield, and Greenbush on the Hudson River. It followed that river north through Half-Moon and Saratoga to Fort Edward. The whole journey took about seventeen arduous days.[37]

Nicholas worked at Fort Edward about two and a half months. With the first freeze, the Fort closed for the winter with plans to reopen when the ice broke up in the spring. Mr. Bowes left about the first of December, going down the Hudson to "Salatog Fort," Still Water Fort, and Albany; across the river to Greenbush, Half-Way House, Canterhook, and Stone House; back into Massachusetts at Sheffield; through Glasgo to Westfield and Springfield, where he crossed the Connecticut River, and through Brexford to Western, a town now called Warren.

In Western Mr. Bowes was stricken.

The Reverend Ebenezer Parkman, of Westborough, heard about the tragedy almost immediately. "I was much interrupted," he wrote on December 13, "by the coming of Captain Thomas Stoddard from Fort Edward. He tells me he supposes Mr. Bowes, late of Bedford, one of the chaplains in the army, to be by this time dead, he having been struck suddenly by numb palsey, and speechless when he was with him as he came down upon his journey. May God grant that I myself be always ready! Since we know not the day nor the hour." On the fourteenth, Mr. Parkman continued: "Reverend Mr. Bowes death is in several ways confirmed . . . in the afternoon on the occasion of Mr. Bowes death, I repeated the remainder of what I began on occasion of Deacon Newton's sudden death last February, viz. from Deut. 32,29 'O that they were wise, that they understood this, that they would consider their latter end!' "[38]

Clerical and military leaders gathered in Bedford on December 18, expecting the burial of Nicholas Bowes. Ebenezer Bridge, of

Fig. 21. Tombstone of the Reverend Mr. Nicholas Bowes, at
Warren, Massachusetts (1971 photograph)

Chelmsford Church, wrote in his diary that a message had been sent to them: the body of Nicholas Bowes would not be brought home.

Indeed, Lucy Bowes had made other arrangements. When Mr. Bowes was stricken, he was taken to the home of the Reverend Isaac Jones in Western. He was buried where he fell, in Western, in the Jones's lot, directly in back of the space reserved for Mr. Jones himself. A gravestone was ordered from a local artisan, William Young, of Tatnuck.[39]

The slate Mr. Young used was of poor quality, thinly layered and easily chipped. In places it broke away as he worked on it, and he recut the letters. Then he misspelled the name on the headstone,* but not on the footstone. At the top of the slate he designed a stylized portrait of a New England clergyman in his wig and a feathered cloak, under which he cut the personal epitaph, which Lucy Bowes may have written:

Here lyes interred the
Remains of the Revd Mr.
NICHOLAS BOEWS
Late Pastor of the Church
of Christ in Bedford; who
having been egaged as
chaplain in the Army at the
westward upon his Return
was violently seized with
his last illness in this place
and suddenly Departed
this life Decemr 12th AD 1755
in the 50th year of his age

It is not known whether Lucy rode to Western to see her husband's grave, whether she knew about the flaking slate and the misspelled name, but she had arranged a noble memorial on top of a gentle hill overlooking the peaceful New England countryside for the Reverend Mr. Nicholas Bowes.

---

* He also misspelled the common word *engaged*.

III

✎§ THE REVEREND
MR. NATHANIEL SHERMAN ৡ

There may have been many reasons why Lucy Bowes did not bring
her husband's body home to Bedford for burial. Certainly she must
have been rankled by the situation which caused his resignation.
Moreover, she may have felt the occasion of a burial would reopen
the townsmen's wounds, dividing them into two groups, some paying respect to the dead while others ignored the event.

Recently, a candidate for the pulpit, a young man Lucy could
not bring herself to invite to the burial, had come to live at the
home of James Lane, Jr. He was Nathaniel Sherman. He had arrived
while Mr. Bowes was composing his resignation, and had been
preaching in the meetinghouse for four months. Nathaniel was
twenty-nine, a little older than many young men seeking first pulpits,
for he had struggled to prepare for his profession, and that had
taken time.

His father William had been a cordwainer who had moved
around the Province. After his first wife died, William had married
Mehitabel Wellington, and they had four sons, William, Roger,*
Nathaniel, and Josiah, and three daughters. Nathaniel was born in
that part of Dorchester which was to become Stoughton. Three
years later Josiah was born in Newton.

Nathaniel had been fourteen and Josiah eleven when George
Whitefield had visited Newton. The impact upon the town had
been total: every inhabitant held an opinion about his work. His
supporters were ardent, while his opponents were certain that his

---

* Later to sign the Declaration of Independence.

influence was evil. After his departure, a converted layman named Nathan Ward carried on "the work." Usually townsmen did not tax their minister, but Newton's men did tax Mr. Ward because they knew he was neither educated for nor ordained to the ministry.

In this atmosphere both Nathaniel and Josiah were inspired to preach as Whitefield did. The way must have seemed difficult, and it became worse, when their father died a year after the evangelist's visit.

Their brother William was keeping store in Milford, Connecticut, and as soon as it could be arranged the family moved there.

Nathaniel was twenty when a charter was granted for a school to open in Elizabethtown, New Jersey, for training New Light ministers. A group of Presbyterians in New York and New Jersey had applied for the charter because they were dissatisfied with the preparation for the ministry young men of their faith were receiving. They believed a conscious awareness of God's spirit was a requirement for all ministers as well as for all members of a church, and they wanted a school which would teach New Light techniques. In this they were encouraged by George Whitefield.

The first president of the school was the Presbyterian minister of Elizabethtown, Jonathan Dickinson. Classes were held in his home and the school library was his personal library. However, Mr. Dickinson lived only a few months and was succeeded by the Presbyterian minister of Newark, Aaron Burr. Mrs. Burr was the daughter of Jonathan Edwards, of Northhampton, Massachusetts.[1]

Mr. Burr moved the school to his home in Newark. Because the school lacked funds, he drew no salary from it and served not only as president, but also as professor, secretary, librarian, and purchasing agent.

Nathaniel and Josiah Sherman were not required to become Presbyterians to enroll in the school, but they were to have knowledge of Latin and Greek. Nathaniel entered in 1749, and Josiah a year later. Their classes met with Mr. Burr or a tutor. The days opened and closed with prayer and Bible readings. They lived in Mr. Burr's home or in rented quarters in a private home near-by. Their rooms contained a shelf; a table with a candle, quill, paper, and ink; a chest; a chair or two; and a cot-like bed. On Sabbaths they attended either Mr. Burr's services in Newark or other public worship services. They were fined four pence for not attending at all.

The student body may have been as large as fifty men when Nathaniel was graduated in 1753. During Josiah's last year at the school plans were made for the first building, which was completed in 1756. It was named Nassau Hall after the House of Nassau, the family of King William the Third. Today it is Princeton University.[2]

While Nathaniel was still in school, his cousin, Mary Wellington,[3] of Lexington, and James Lane, Jr., of Bedford, were married. In 1754 James's cousin, Stephen Minot, and his uncle, Timothy Minot, had been brought in to preach in the Bedford meetinghouse. With the dismissal of Mr. Bowes, Mary Lane knew that pulpit was vacant and she also knew that there was an opening in Woburn for a colleague to the blind and aging John Fox. This was an opportunity for both her cousins. While Nathaniel was boarding with her, Josiah applied in Woburn.

Bedford's townsmen were paying Nathaniel £1 a week while he supplied the pulpit. But they were restless and they reminded the church that a contract should be drawn for a permanent minister. After six more weeks had passed, Nathaniel Sherman's name finally was sent forward by the church and accepted by the town with 38 ayes.* By then, Nicholas Bowes was preaching at Fort Edward.

Nathaniel must have noticed the close ties in the community when the town's committee brought a proposed contract to him. The men named to treat with him were James Lane Jr.'s uncle, Deacon Job; his cousin, Nathaniel Page; his brother-in-law, Benjamin Hutchinson, Jr.; a man being trained for the deaconship, Stephen Davis; and Deacon Israel Putnam. They offered him £53 6s 8d as an annual salary, £113 6s 8d as a settlement fee, and twenty cords of wood each year "after he shall come to need it for his own firring."[4]

Nathaniel accepted without bargaining.** His contract was approved by the town on December 15, 1755, three days after the death of Nicholas Bowes.

---

* The nays were not recorded.

** Nathaniel Sherman's signature as traced from the town clerk's record book in Bedford:

Fig. 22. Hugh Maxwell's tombstone (from a 1971 rubbing)

Mr. Sherman's ordination was planned for January 21, 1756, and his brother Josiah, who had been accepted in Woburn, was to be ordained on January 28. This may have been awkward, for Nathaniel's ceremony was postponed until February 18. The program is not known, but it is probable that delegates from each church were council members for the ceremonies in the respective meeting-houses.

The five committeemen in charge of Nathaniel's service entertained the guests in their own homes, receiving a little more than a pound each as the town's expense. By that time, Mr. Sherman had preached twenty six Sabbaths and one fast and one thanksgiving service.

Nathaniel was unmarried and did not need his firewood. He allowed the townsmen to substitute whatever they wished in its place. He received £2 a year when wood was 3s 4d a cord, or about £3 7s for twenty cords. When he did decide to marry, he chose Deacon Nathaniel Merriam's granddaughter Lydia. They were to live on the road to Bedford's spring near Lydia's sister Anna and her husband, Thomas Page. The townsmen voted to carry the wood to Nathaniel's house before January 1, 1759.

During that winter, Nathaniel fell ill and found a substitute for the pulpit for two or three weeks. For this expense, the townsmen granted him £2 13s 4d. As soon as he was well, he and Lydia were married. It was March 1, 1759, and the groom was thirty-four. Lydia was to be seventeen in April. Josiah of Woburn was already married, having chosen a niece of Martha (Minot) Lane, Martha Minot, of Concord.

Shortly after the wedding, a pew owner, Hugh Maxwell, fell from a horse and was killed. The influence of Mr. Sherman's New Light teaching was seen in the epitaph cut on the tombstone of the pious man:[5]

HERE LYES THE BODY OF

MR. HUGH MAXUEL HE DE-

PARTED THIS LIFE MARCH 19

1759 IN THE 59 YEAR OF HIS AGE

MY BODY TURNED INTO DUST

MY DUST IT SHALL ARISE

IN RESURECTION OF THE JUST

TO SOUND JEHOVAHS PRAISE

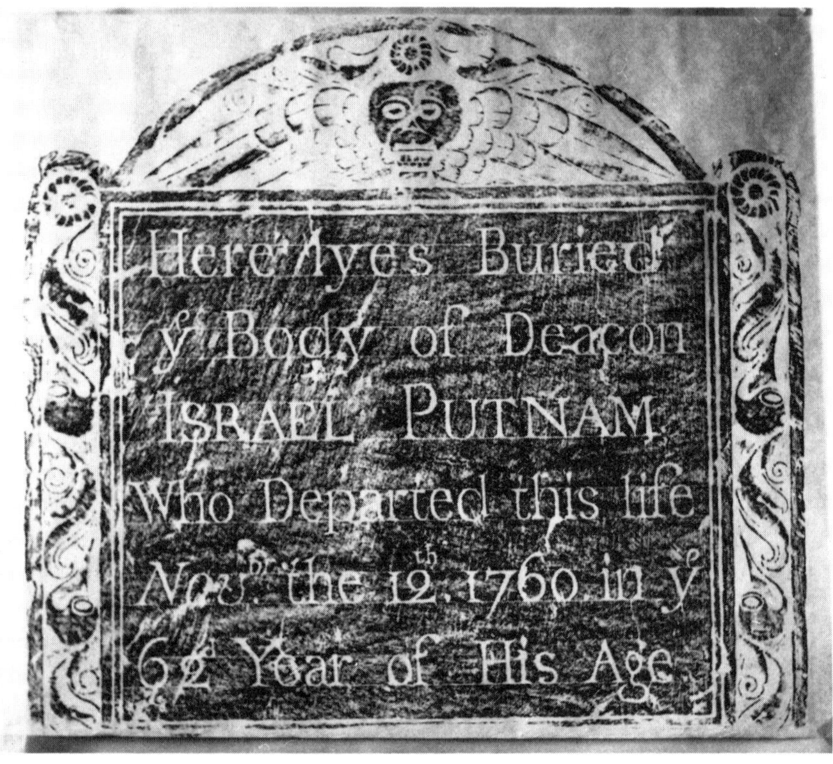

Fig. 23. Deacon Israel Putnam's tombstone (from a 1971 rubbing)

George Whitefield often spoke about the dust from which God had created Adam and of the dust in which the dead slept, waiting for "the trump . . . to sound." He taught that both the body and the soul were refashioned for heaven in the resurrection of the Elect.

Hugh Maxwell Jr. was married that year, and when his first child was born, the infant was carried to the meetinghouse for baptism. The parents became full members of the church on the same day.

When the church was thirty years old, the deacons Israel Putnam and Job Lane had grown infirm, and they resigned. Benjamin Bacon, forty-six, husband of Catherine (Lane), was named in Israel's place; he was to hold that office for thirty two years. Stephen Davis, forty-five, who had served on many town committees for the church, was elected to Deacon Lane's chair. Stephen had two daughters, Lydia and Dorcas, who may have been named for Lydia and Dorcas Bowes. He also had one son, Thaddeus.

The first infant born to the Shermans was named Nathaniel after his father and his great-grandfather, Deacon Nathaniel Merriam. Their second child was a boy called Thaddeus, the name of Deacon Davis's son. Their third child was a girl named Lydia, the name of the baby's mother and of one of Deacon Davis's daughters.

Shortly after he resigned, Deacon Israel Putnam died. The two new deacons were appointed committeemen to appraise his estate, valued at £444.[6] His headstone bore no reference to dust. It was worded in the simple dignity of an earlier day.

Here lyes Buried
ye Body of Deacon
ISRAEL PUTNAM
Who Departed this life
Novbr the 12th, 1760, in ye
62d Year of His Age.

Two years later, Deacon Job Lane was laid under one fashioned in the same quiet manner:

Fig. 24. Colonel John Lane's tombstone (from a 1971 rubbing)

Memento mori
Here lies the Body of
Deacon JOB LANE
who departed this
Life August the 9th
A.D. 1762 in the 74th
Year of his Age

However, when Colonel John Lane died, a verse expressing New Light teaching was chiseled on his tombstone:

Memento mori
Here lies the Body of
CoLLl JOHN LANE
of Bedford who died
Sept the 23th AD 1763
in the 72d year of his Age.
While I lye buried deep in dust my flesh
shall be thy care
These withering limbs with the I trust to rais
them strong & fair

The New Light tenet was clear. Whitefield himself had asked his audience, "Do ye not long for the time when ye shall have new bodies, when they shall be immortal, and made like Christ's glorious body . . ."[7] New Light expressions were becoming perfect in form and they would be declared for many years.

Bedford Church was growing at the rate of about five new members a year, but baptisms were falling from the thirteen or fourteen performed each year by Mr. Bowes to an average of seven annually under Mr. Sherman. His sermons were probably colorful and effective. In Woburn, when his brother preached, "his elocution was distinct, tho' fluent and rapid. His voice was excellent. His mind was discriminating. His eloquence was often pathetic, sometimes powerful, and always of such character as to command the respect and attention of his audience."[8] Often the word "pathetic" described New Light sermons of this period. Josiah Sherman was eloquent, and Nathaniel is believed to have been equally talented.

All townsmen accepted the Congregational method of deciding policies whereby every church member had a right to vote on matters of the church and every taxable inhabitant had a right to vote in town affairs. But in religious philosophy the inhabitants were divided. New Light teachings were not all-pervading in the town. Earlier in the year of Colonel Lane's death, both the daughter-in-law and the granddaughter of Daniel Davis died, probably of a contagious disease. For them the epitaphs were quiet:

Memento Mori
Here lyes the Body of
Mrs Elizabeth Davis the
wife of Mr. Josiah Davis
who departed this Life
January the 15th: AD 1763
Aged 41 years 9 months
and 2 days

Memento mori
Here lyes the Body of
Mrs Mary Davis the wife
of Mr Elezer Davis who
departed this Life
January ye 28th AD 1763
Aged 22 years 10 months
and 20 days
Daughter of Mr. Josiah
and Mrs Elizabeth Davis

For them, no mention was made of dust or of a literal resurrection. There was a philosophical division between the Davises and Colonel John Lane.

Deacon Benjamin Bacon's brother John, who owned a part of a pew in the meetinghouse, lived to be forty-three. He died when Benjamin had been a deacon for fifteen months. Yet John's headstone was cut with simple words:

Here lyes Buried
the Body of Mr.
John Bacon,
who Departed this life
May ye 26th 1760 in ye
44th Year of his Age.

The division in leading families of the church was more and more evident.

Nathaniel's health soon became a public concern. The townsmen voted to pay substitute ministers for a month in June 1762, and again in 1764, because of his indisposition. By 1765, the townsmen accepted his frailty and they allowed him an additional £10 for the coming year to provide for his substitutes.

Perhaps little Thaddeus Sherman was not strong, because he died when he was two and a half. The headstone his parents selected was similar to that of Thomas Bowes:

Here lyes ye Body of
Thaddeus Sherman Son
of the Revd. Mr. Nathaniel
Sherman & Mrs. Lydia
his Wife. Who died
Aug. ye 22 1765 Aged
2 Years & 5 Months

(Fig. 25)

It did not speak of dust, resurrection, and the grave, because New Lights could not imagine their infants rejected and cast aside. Whitefield had said he did not believe that any infants were damned in hell. Infants or children too young for religious experiences were excused from the rigors of the philosophy.

That fall (1765) the churchmen, under Mr. Sherman's guidance, voted to have only one church covenant, abolishing the Half-Way Covenant and the privilege of half-membership. They felt, as many in the Province did, that half-members had not grown in holiness as had been expected, nor had they applied for full membership and

Fig. 25. Thaddeus Sherman's tombstone (from a 1971 rubbing)

the rite of communion. Their presence in the group diluted the piety of the whole.

The unity of all the churches had become diffuse in the face of this dilemma. Some had cast aside piety and opened both ordinances to all persons who appeared to walk well, hoping participation in the rites would help them to learn holiness. Others had adopted the Half-Way Covenant in theory, but had not practiced it, preferring to cling to the original meaning of a church as a group of saints in full communion with one another and with God.

In Bedford the church was returning to this latter concept because the members voted that henceforth those applying to join were to be examined by the minister several days before their admission. They were expected to be holy and repentant, to believe in Christ and the Catechism of the Westminster Assembly in England. After they had passed their examination, Mr. Sherman would send their names to the church. If there were no objections among the members, they would be admitted without a vote.

With no half-membership, a baptism would be performed only for full members, and the ministerial examination would prevent the admission of hypocrites. Because baptisms had diminished under Mr. Sherman, apparently he had not encouraged the rite, although he would perform it.

The question of baptism for the unconverted became a topic of family debate, and the discussion impressed Thaddeus Davis, son of the deacon, a boy nearly twelve. It included the case of the newborn, and Thaddeus decided small children were not properly prepared for the ordinance and should not be subjected to it by adults. Only those with religious experience were qualified. So when Thaddeus grew up, he married Sarah Stearns, niece of Josiah Stearns, who had often preached in Bedford; and drove to Woburn to attend a Baptist church. Later he was named a deacon, and he was given an annual rebate on his ministerial tax in Bedford since he was paying one elsewhere.

Lydia Sherman's youngest brother, William Merriam, fifteen, also was bent toward the Baptist tenet by the controversy in Bedford. He was to attend a Baptist school, but he remained in the Bedford church where his confusion was to become a problem both in the church and the town.

The townsmen were dissatisfied with the new church covenant, and they neglected, in March 1766, to vote the funds for Mr. Sherman's substitute. By September there was a deficit of £13 6s 8d, because substitutes had been paid, but the townsmen refused to grant additional funds for preaching.

With this rebuff, Nathaniel Sherman refused to preach at all.

By late October, the townsmen were asked how they wished to supply the pulpit inasmuch as the Reverend Mr. Nathaniel Sherman had neglected and still refused to preach. They voted to pay for preaching for one Sabbath and to adjourn for a week to consider the situation.

At week's end, they said they would have preaching for three weeks and carefully named a committee to find a supply for the pulpit. Obed Abbott, sixty-nine, the only remaining original covenantor; John Lane, forty-eight, son of the original covenantor, Deacon Job; Nathaniel Page, sixty-four, son of the original covenantor Nathaniel and Susanna (Lane) Page, were the committeemen. In naming these men, the townsmen seemed to stress a return to the form of covenant and church they had known.

In the midst of these troubles, Jonathan Woolley, the town's messenger at the time of the Nicholas Bowes problem, suddenly died. He was sixty-four and he either fell from a stone wall or into a hole near a road. He left a vacant pew in the meetinghouse.

Supplies for the pulpit were temporary and within a month the church held a council meeting with its neighboring churches, seeking advice. The members of the council and the number of days it sat are not known. The townsmen allowed 9s per day for entertaining the male members, except for Isaac Barron,* and 6 for the women. The council advised the church to dismiss Nathaniel Sherman, which the church agreed to do.

On December 12, 1766, with Obed Abbott moderating the meeting, the townsmen concurred and voted to give Mr. Sherman "the whole of his firewood and salary for the present year notwithstanding his dismission." [9]

Nathaniel Sherman accepted the pulpit in the Church of Christ, Mount Carmel (now Hamden), Connecticut, near New Haven,

---

* Why the women got less and who Isaac Barron was is not explained in the Bedford town records, May 21, 1767.

where his brother Roger was living.[10] He broke up his farm of about one hundred and twenty acres and sold it in small pieces to various townsmen, keeping five acres for himself until three years before his death.

While the Shermans were moving away from the neighborhood of Lydia's sister and brother-in-law, her father died. His tombstone spelled out the promise it is believed Nathaniel taught:

Memento mori
Here lies Buried
the Body of
Lieut John Meriam,
who died Sept. 20th
1767. In the 67th year
of his Age.
But Christ shall Change my sinful Dust
The grave shall rot off all my rust
This body of mine shall fashon'd be
Like to his own in its degree.

(Fig. 26)

For Mr. Sherman's installation service at Mount Carmel, the Reverend Naphtali Daggett, of Yale College, preached on "The Great Importance of Speaking in the Most Intelligible Manner in the Christian Church." Perhaps Mr. Daggett thought Nathaniel had been misunderstood in Bedford. But at Mount Carmel Nathaniel also canceled the Half-Way Covenant, and for that he was dismissed.

In 1778, Nathaniel sold his property in Mount Carmel for £600. He loaned the money to the Continental Congress, hoping the interest would be an annual income.[11] He moved to East Windsor, Connecticut, where Joseph was born in 1780 and Anna in 1787. The church in East Windsor had cleansed itself in 1765 when admission of halfway members was set aside. None were afterward admitted to the church except those who gave evidence of being regenerate persons. At last Nathaniel and a church were in harmony, but it is not clear that he ever had a pulpit there.

The Continental Congress ceased paying interest to Nathaniel in 1782 and repaid his capital with notes for one hundred dollars,

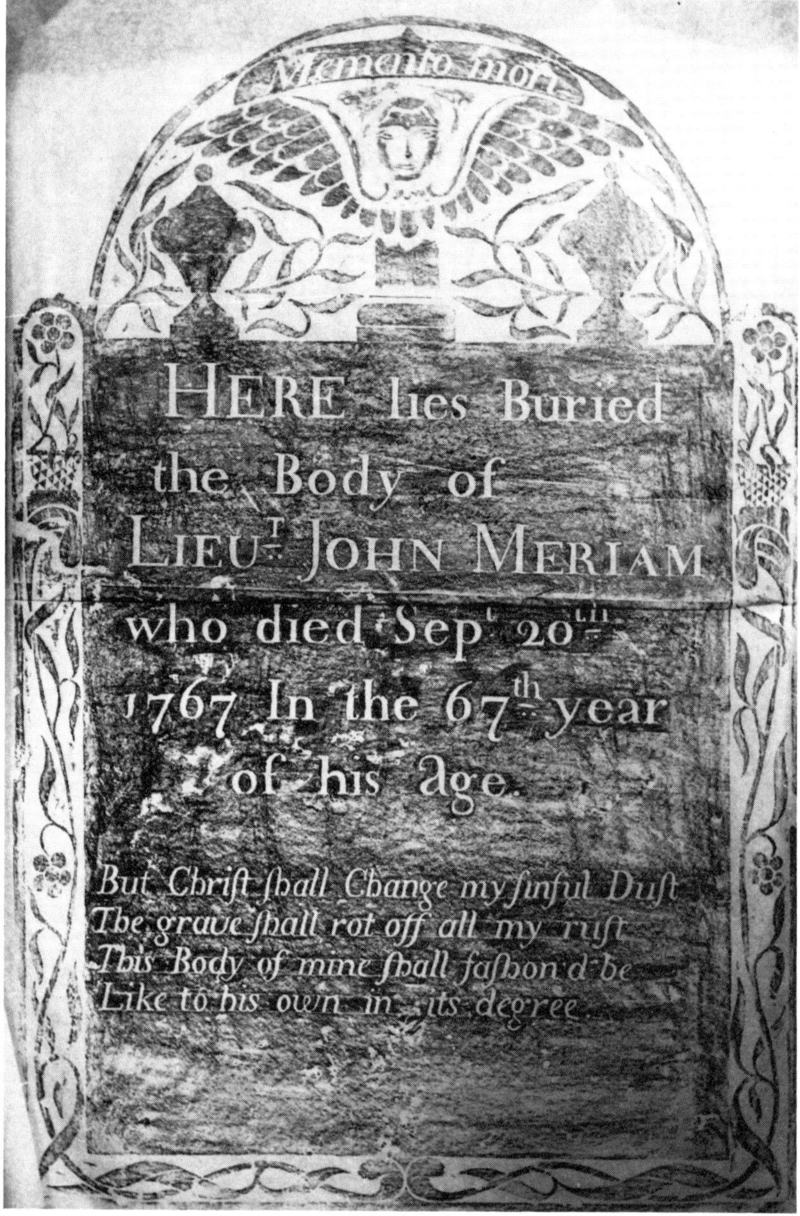

Fig. 26. Lieutenant John Merriam's tombstone (from a 1971
rubbing)

which he loaned to the State of Connecticut without receiving provision for its return. In 1787, at the age of sixty-one, he petitioned the state for payments of interest, a gratuity, or permission to ask for support from his surrounding towns. He was in ill health, infirm, unable to work, and without credit. Erastus Wolcot, Esquire, and the Honorable Roger Sherman, his brother, supported his request and he was granted an annual income from the state.

Two of the children, Joseph and Anna, died in October 1788, and their brother Nathaniel, twenty-nine, died in 1790. Their mother followed, at fifty, in 1793. Their epitaphs had these words:

In Memory of Mr Nathaniel
Sherman Jr, who Died Sept 24th
AD 1790 in ye 30th Year
of his Age He was Exemplay*
For Sobriety & Faithfulness &
was a Skilful Instructor of
Youth near 12 Years.
Near him lies his Brother
Joseph who Died Octobr 14th
1788 in his 8th Year.
And his Sister Anna, who Died
Octor 4th 1788: Aged 10 Mont
& 10 Days. The Children of
The Rev [d] Nathl & Mrs
[Nathaniel?] Sherman.

(Fig. 27)

---

* The letter *r* was added later to give this word the correct spelling.

Fig. 27. The tombstone of Nathaniel, Jr., Joseph, and Anna Sherman, at South Windsor, Connecticut (1971 photograph)

Fig. 28. Lydia Sherman's tombstone, at South Windsor,
Connecticut (1971 photograph)

In Memory of Mrs
LYDIA SHERMAN
the Virtuous & amiable
Consort of the Revd
Nathaniel Sherman
Who Died Febr 3d
AD 1793 in ye 51st
Year of her
Age.
Early the Christian
Race She Run
And Soon a Crown
of Glory Won.

(Fig. 28)

Nathaniel Sherman lived four more years after the death of his wife, and died at seventy-one, in July 1797. The daughter, Lydia, who was now thirty-two and had been born in Bedford, was the only remaining member of the family.*

The Shermans were buried in the Old, or Hill, Cemetery near the Connecticut River in South Windsor. Lydia Sherman may have arranged her father's biographical tombstone. Cut on coarse white marble, it has no design, motif, or border of vines. It is a simple white stone covered with lettering.

---

* This does not take into account the possibility of children having been born at Mount Carmel.

In
memory of the
Revd Nathaniel Sherman AM
He was born at Stoughton in Massachusetts
March 2 AD 1726:
was educated at Princeton College
and graduated in 1752.
He soon after entered on the work of
the Gospel Ministry;
was ordained pastor of the Church &
Society in Bedford. Massachusetts.
and afterwards for severel years was the
Pastor of the first Church & Society in Hamdem
He was ever fond of the study of divinity
skilful faithful & zealous in his calling: a
true Calvinist; a fervent Preacher, a pious man
After enduring, for years an uncommon share of
bodily infirmities, which he bore with Christian
fortitude. He died at East Windsor
July. 18. 1797
Æ 71.

(Fig. 29)

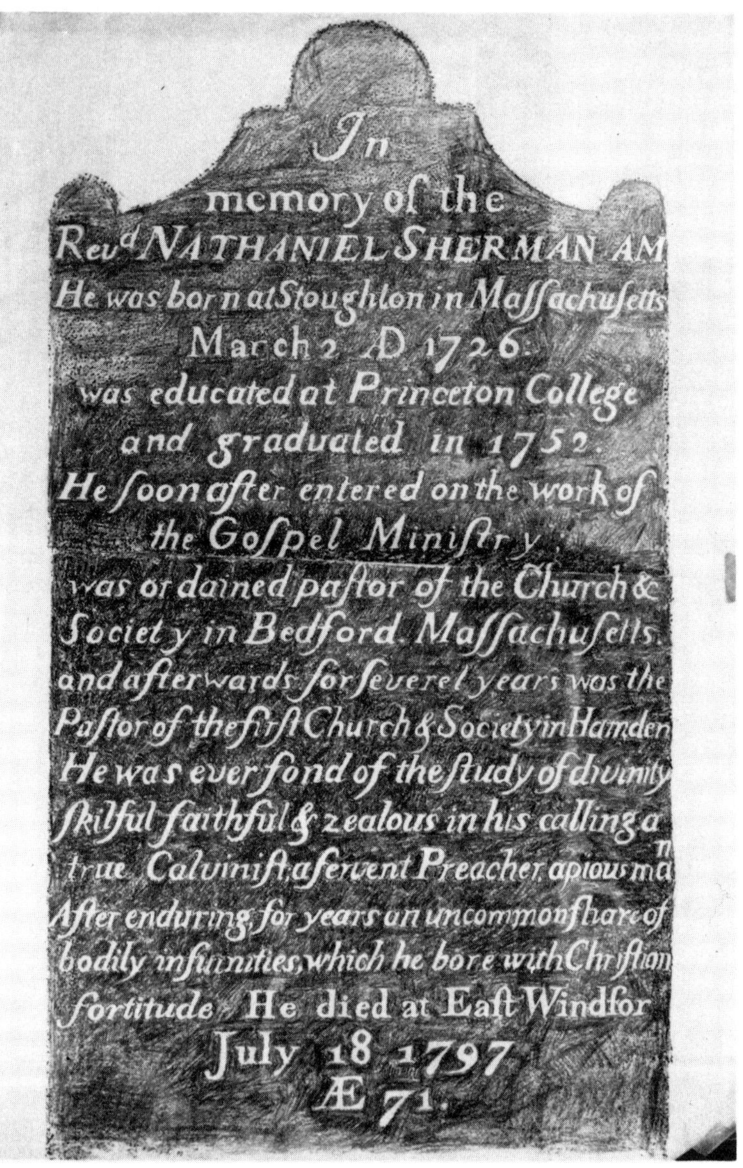

Fig. 29. Tombstone of the Reverend Nathaniel Sherman, in the Old Cemetery at South Windsor, Connecticut (from a 1971 rubbing)

IV

After Mr. Sherman's dismissal, all the voters of Bedford, for the elect group of churchmen were townsmen, had to keep the pulpit supplied while they mended a meetinghouse thirty-seven years old and repaired the theological climate of the church for the benefit of everyone. Secular matters were easily decided upon. The townsmen voted £30 then £50 to defray the charges of pulpit supplies by reason of the circumstances of the town while they also named a committee to shingle the meetinghouse. The work was done in the spring of 1767 with 18-inch shingles laid five and a half inches to the weather.

Two years passed before the churchmen found a likely candidate for the pulpit, in Isaac Thacher, a graduate of Nassau Hall. He was actively seeking a pulpit, as he had been out of school for seven years. Unfortunately, he had accepted the pulpit in Gorham, either in Maine or in New Hampshire, before the invitation from Bedford's townsmen reached him.

Then the church heard Joseph Willard for five and a half months before naming him, by 22 votes, a candidate. Mr. Willard, son of Benjamin and Sarah (Brooks) Willard, of Grafton, Massachusetts, and a Harvard graduate, was descended from Simon Willard, a trader who had worked in the 1630's with Peter Bulkeley to settle the town of Concord.

The townsmen offered Mr. Willard £66 a year and a settlement of £120, adding that his salary would be cut in half each year he remained in the pastoral office but was unable to preach. Mr. Willard's health is not known, but he lived eighty years, and worked in two pulpits. He would not accept the restriction on salary, and the townsmen quarreled about his allotment of firewood, voting 25 to 25 as to whether he should have any. So they dropped Mr. Willard.* He was ordained in Mendon, Massachusetts, where he became known as a Universalist, and later he preached in Boxborough.

The church, having failed to seat a New Light because he was not available and having failed to elect a Universalist because of a quarrel over his firewood, looked at their covenant and searched for a candidate with more general appeal. They rewrote the covenant, keeping the concept of a pious church, but restoring the privilege of baptism to all who walked well. "This church," they agreed, "shall have but one covenant, and therefore require the same qualifications in all; yet if any person desire to enter into covenant and receive baptism for himself or children, and yet fears to approach the Lord's table at present, he shall be received, he promising (though he come not immediately to the Lord's table) that he will submit himself to the watch and discipline of this church." [1]

This statement was remarkable since it not only permitted baptism to everyone, but granted full membership to the baptized even if they were too humble or meek to share in the Lord's supper. Henceforth the church would be larger, a group of both baptized and regenerate persons.

The change was accepted immediately in the town, and while the church was without a permanent minister, twenty-eight townsmen were baptized by visiting clerics and seven joined those taking communion. The baptisms were nearly as many as Nathaniel Sherman had performed in five years.

During the winter of 1768–69, the church heard Thomas Abbott, Daniel Johnson, John Moore, Ephraim Ward, and John Emerson. All were graduates of Harvard College. Thomas Abbott was later ordained in West Roxbury, where he worked ten years before he was dismissed. Daniel Johnson became minister in the town of Harvard and was a chaplain during the Revolutionary War. John (Jonathan) Moore was first the College librarian and then had the pulpit in Rochester, Massachusetts, where he preached two years before he was dismissed for his liberal views. Ephraim Ward ministered in Brookfield, Massachusetts, for forty-seven years, following the Cove-

---

* His four brothers, Benjamin, Simon, Ephraim and Aaron were famous clockmakers.

nant of Grace and teaching godliness. He was sincere, amiable, and pious; he avoided disputes and refused to support any ecclesiastical party.

The majority of the church wanted John Emerson as a candidate for the pulpit. But the minority were so unhappy at this prospect that "for peace sake, a young candidate newly begun to preach"[2] was hired for a month. He was Asa Dunbar, twenty-four, of Bridgewater, a recent Harvard graduate, who was to preach in Salem seven years before he was dismissed. He left the ministry, moved to Keene, New Hampshire, and practiced law. Later his daughter became Henry David Thoreau's mother.

In September 1769, the townsmen concurred with the church in offering the pulpit to John Emerson.

John was the son of Mary (Moody) Emerson and the Reverend Joseph Emerson, of Malden, a minister who had arranged, in 1744, to have Whitefield preach in his pulpit. John's brother William had accepted Daniel Bliss's New Light pulpit in Concord and had married Daniel's daughter Phoebe. Although his brother would be near-by, John did not want Bedford's pulpit or any around the Bay. He went to Conway, Massachusetts, a frontier community far from ecclesiastical differences. He said he would be "John, preaching in the wilderness."[3] In old age, he wrote that he had adopted doctrines called Calvinistic and had preached the tenet of human depravity, regeneration, justification, repentance, and faith to all his people.

Once more the church turned to supplies, hearing Jacob Bigelow, Andrew Elliot, Timothy Hilliard, Samuel Hunt, and Amos Sawyer.

Mr. Hunt has not been identified, and Mr. Sawyer died before he had been paid, but the first three were young Harvard graduates. Mr. Bigelow, an affable and social man, soon was ordained in a precinct church in Sudbury, where Whitefield had not been admitted. Mr. Elliot, after working as librarian and tutor at the College, went to Fairfield, Connecticut, to preach. Mr. Hilliard became Nathaniel Appleton's colleague in Cambridge Church. He did not handle "subjects of doubtful disputation, knowing that they generally tend in vain jangling, rather than in godly edifying."[4] He has been considered an early Unitarian.

The town began to rely on its schoolteacher, Jacob Coogin, originally of Woburn, to fill the pulpit. But finally, six years after the dismissal of Mr. Sherman, the church by a vote of 31 to 29, and the town by a majority of 46 votes called Joseph Penniman, thirty-four, of the town of Braintree, to Bedford's pulpit. They offered him £66 13s 4d as an annual salary and £133 6s 8d as a settlement, and they asked two sons of the original covenantors and John Reed, who had moved to Bedford from Lexington and had bought the Bowes's estate from the widow Lucy and her family, to treat with Mr. Penniman. Joseph accepted the offer in 1771 and became Bedford's third minister.*

Braintree was a large area divided into three districts. The first meetinghouse had been built in the north part, now Quincy, and Lucy Bowes's brother, John Hancock, had preached there. It also had an Episcopal church. Joseph had been born in the middle part, which is still called Braintree. During his boyhood, the church had been Calvinistic, and in 1771 Ezra Weld was its minister. The third parish in the south was composed of what today are Holbrook and Randolph. So Joseph had grown up where there were both New and Old Light churches as well as an Episcopal one.

He was the son of William and Ruth (Thayer) Penniman, born on October 5, 1737. He could scarcely remember a year when his father was not serving on a town committee. Would William Penniman examine the treasurer's book? Would he find a way to prevent people carrying stones away from the common? Would he serve as constable? as tithingman? as moderator? as selectman? Would he order the middle school? Clear the way for the fish-run up the river? Change Iron Works Bridge to County Bridge? Store the town's powder? Help divide the common? Petition for a provincial line between Abington and Bridgewater? Petition to have Suffolk County divided? Joseph's father worked diligently for the benefit of all his fellow townsmen.

William's brother and Joseph's uncle, James, was a deacon of the middle church. He, too, worked for the whole community. Would he ask the General Court for the cost of the highways? Would he tell the representative how the town wished to deal with the Stamp Act (1765)? Would he wait on the ministers of the several congregations, asking them to announce next Sabbath that the selectmen were calling a day of prayer on Tuesday, October 4, 1769? And would he ask them to "address the Supreme Governor of

---

* Joseph's signature as traced from the town clerk's record book in Bedford:

the universe in a social as well as a private manner, for the removing the Evils they feel as also averting those they fear?"[5] The senior Pennimans were accustomed to diversified congregations and served all of them.

Joseph was twenty-four when he entered Harvard College. The school had grown and changed since Mr. Bowes's undergraduate days. It was so crowded that ninety students lodged in town. The students met in a chapel for daily prayers, but on Sabbaths they continued to go to Cambridge meetinghouse for services led by Nathaniel Appleton. While Joseph was at the College, Old Harvard Hall burned, destroying the entire library. Whitefield, on his sixth journey to America, heard of this when he was in Concord, Massachusetts. He gave "some useful puritanical books" toward a new library.

The physical science courses had diversified. Work had been done in the fields of electricity, earthquakes, the transit of Venus, and Halley's comet. When the cause of earthquakes was traced to stress in the earth itself, it became clear the tremblings were not the result of God shaking the ground to punish His sinful and disobedient provincials. The concept of God changed and the ministry, the churches, and the congregations once more recognized His gracious quality of protective care.

The students staged plays in College Hall and once were punished for presenting what may have been a satire on the Judgment Day, since they enacted the awful events, and one played the part of the Devil.

For the graduation of fifty-five students in 1765, when Joseph completed his courses, one graduate spoke on the question, "Can new prohibitory duties which make it useless for the people to engage in commerce be evaded by them as faithful subjects?" concluding that the faithful could evade the duties.[6]

Joseph was at the College in 1768–69 studying for his Master's degree. He could have known twelve of the men[7] who preached in Bedford's vacant pulpit and could have known of the rift in the town. But because of the example in his family, and because he respected the beliefs of others, he must have felt that he could work there nonetheless.

Before Joseph moved to Bedford, George Whitefield died in Newburyport, Massachusetts. He was on his seventh journey and had preached in twenty towns before he succumbed. Pallbearers came from Portsmouth, Newbury, Newburyport, and Rowley. The preacher was buried in the town where he died, under a biographical tombstone:

THIS CENOTAPH
is erected with affectionate veneration,
to the memory of the
REV. GEORGE WHITEFIELD
born at Gloucester, Eng. Dec'r. 16, 1714:
educated at Oxford University; ordained 1736.
In a ministry of thirty-four years, he crossed the Atlantic thirteen
times, and preached more than eighteen thousand sermons.
As a soldier of the cross, humble, devout, ardent; he put on
the whole armor of God, preferring the honors of Christ
to his own interest, repose, reputation, or life. As a
Christian orator, his deep piety, disinterested zeal,
and vivid imagination, gave unexampled energy
to his look, action, and utterance. Bold, fervent, pungent, and popular in his eloquence,
no other uninspired man ever preached to so
large assemblies, or enforced the simple
truths of the gospel by motives so per-
suasive and awful, and with an influence so powerful on the hearts
of his hearers.
He died of asthma, Sept. 30, 1770;
suddenly exchanging his life of unparalleled labors for his
eternal rest.[8]

Joseph Penniman had no relatives in Bedford. When he arrived in March 1771, he boarded with Thomas and Anna (Merriam) Page on the road to the spring, and he stabled his horse there. His ordination was to be on Wednesday, May 21.

The church asked the townsmen to see that the day be "religiously observed, agreeable to the solemnity of the occasion, and that they were determined as much as in them lay to prevent levity, prophaneness, music, dancing, and frolicking and other disorders on said day." They were remembering that Whitefield had said, "they would go to church, but at the same time think it no harm to go to a ball or an assembly, notwithstanding they promised at their baptism, to renounce the pomps and vanities of this wicked world." [9] The townsmen agreed, not only respecting Whitefield's teaching, but wishing to avoid the riotous conditions prevailing near the Bay in the pre-Revolutionary climate.

John Reed, already a leader in town affairs, was proud of the direction being taken by the church and wished it to be accepted in the local family of churches. He offered to entertain the ordaining council and all of Joseph's relatives, if two or three particular churches would be invited to the ordination.

Elizabeth, daughter of Deacon Israel Putnam, and her husband, Elisha Fuller, were John's neighbors in the Deacon's old home. They offered to entertain all visiting clerics and candidates if Mr. Reed's suggestion was adopted.

The town agreed and the visiting council was large. The members were Ezra Weld, from the middle district of Braintree; Samuel Cooke, of West Cambridge, a man who had opposed Whitefield and had taken Widow Lucy Bowes as his second wife; Josiah Sherman, of Woburn, brother of the deposed Nathaniel; Henry Cumings, of Billerica, an Arminian; William Emerson, of Concord, a Calvinist; William Lawrence, of Lincoln; and Jonas Clark, of Lexington, husband of Nicholas Bowes's daughter Lucy. This diverse council reflected the hopes of some townsmen that the church had outgrown ecclesiastical differences and was opening its doors to all, becoming a universal Christian church.

Josiah Sherman opened the ordaining service with prayer. Mr. Weld preached from II Tim. 2:2: "And the things that thou hast heard of me among many witnesses, the same commit thou to faithful men, who shall be able to teach others also." Mr. Cooke gave the charge; Mr. Lawrence extended the right hand of fellowship; and Jonas Clark closed the service with prayer.

John Reed had brought about a service free of doctrine and sectarianism.

Joseph Penniman bought Pollard's inn on thirty-three acres, with house, barn, and sheds, and prepared it for a bride. (Fig. 30) He rode to Plymouth to marry Hannah Jackson on October 10, 1771. Joseph and Hannah lived there for seventeen years, and their five daughters were born in that house.

courtesy the Concord Free Public Library

Fig. 30. First home of the Reverend Mr. Joseph Penniman
in Bedford, which had been Walter Pollard's tavern

The last original covenantor, Obed Abbott, knew of the birth of their first daughter, Hannah, in 1772 before he died. A tombstone was cut in the old way for him and his son, whose body had lain without a stone for seventeen years:

> Here lies Buried
> the Body of
> Mr. Obed Abbott;
> who departed this Life
> May the 11th 1773. in ye
> 77th Year of His Age.
> Also in Memory of Mr. John Abbott;
> who died in ye army at Lake George
> Novbr. ye 2d 1756 Aged 23 Years

The child Hannah had sisters, Molly and Lucy, at three-year intervals. The Pennimans were busy, often boarding John Hancock when he traveled to attend the County Convention and then the Continental Congress sitting in Concord.

In 1773, the townsmen voted to supply hymnals for public worship services, deciding on Watts's Psalms. Probably this was the first use of town's books for individuals. They further standardized the music by naming two men to sit in the foreseat of the front gallery to lead the tune.

Townsmen were also working on the meetinghouse, repairing windows and seats, propping up the building, and cutting drops* for it. They planned to cover it with clapboards, but before that project was commenced, the Revolutionary War had affected the town and repairs were laid aside.

There were two groups of military men among the inhabitants, the regular militia and the recently created Minute Men. Together they were seventy-seven of the eighty-eight male inhabitants between sixteen and sixty years of age. On Tuesday evening, April 18, 1775, they were warned that British troops were marching from the Bay to Concord to seize supplies stored there. Both militay groups hurried to Concord early Wednesday morning, and Nathaniel Page is said to have carried a banner as he marched.** These men were joined

---

* Doric ornaments in the form of droplets.
** The Bedford Flag.

by so many volunteers that almost every able townsman took part in the battle.

Studies have been made showing that before the war, sermons of some ministers were incendiary, encouraging congregations to seek freedom with arms. Moreover, some of the Elect had moved from the concept of a complete resurrection in heaven to the fulfillment of heaven here on earth, with God reigning among them, and they sought to be instruments in hastening the day of the millennium by throwing off the tyranny of a foreign king. Jonathan Edwards himself had described a pre-millennium period of a thousand years during which God would reign on earth before the final judgment leading to a total endless heaven, and his followers believed these were the opening days. Even Josiah Stearns in his pulpit in Epping, New Hampshire, reviewed the causes of war in biblical days and drew the conclusion that the provincials stood on solid ground in resisting the British impositions.

It is not known how far the desire for the millennium or the pre-millennium had spread among the Elect in Bedford, or whether Joseph Penniman ever preached inflammatory sermons. There is no evidence that the march of Bedford's men was a religious crusade. With a neighboring town under attack, love for home was high and almost every man responded. Fifty-five individual members of twenty large families whose names were connected with the church were in the fray.[10] They helped drive the British away, but their success was sober.

The captain of the militia, Jonathan Wilson, was killed, and Job Lane, son of Deacon Job, was wounded. Joseph Penniman prayed at Captain Wilson's burial service, and his prayer caused the first misunderstanding between him and some of the inhabitants:

> "We pray thee, O Lord, to send the British Soldiers
> where they will do some good, for Thou knowest that we
> have no use for them about here." [11]

People who heard his words were ill at ease, feeling he was showing disrespect to God by being too familiar with Him. Joseph seemed to speak as if God were his neighbor. It was a peculiar prayer.

Of course Deacon James Penniman, of Braintree, had been instructed to ask the ministers to address "the Supreme Governor of the universe" in a social as well as in a more private manner, and

Joseph was following that custom. It was a practice he would follow all his life.

The misunderstanding grew a little when some townsmen commented that Mr. Penniman had not ridden to battle with his church and congregation, but had remained at home in prayer. They could have pointed to the example of the Reverend Phillips Payson, of Chelsea, who led a few provincials to an attack on twelve British soldiers carrying supplies for their main force in Concord. Mr. Payson and his men had killed one member of the supply unit, wounded a few, and captured the remainder with their arms and supplies.[12] Mr. Payson was a loyal provincial. Could it be that Mr. Penniman leaned toward the Tories?

Joseph was busy with clerical work. Two fasts and one thanksgiving had been called in 1774, and three fasts and a thanksgiving in 1775. On Wednesday, July 3, 1776, he was a guest in John Marrett's pulpit in Burlington for a lecture day held because of drought and war. Joseph preached from Ps. 39:9 "I was dumb, I opened not my mouth, because Thou didst it." The next day Mr. Penniman was host for Bedford's lecture day when William Emerson, of Concord, prayed and preached and John Marrett gave the final prayer. A week later Joseph preached in the afternoon in Concord for an all-day fast. The following Sabbath Mr. Penniman, Mr. Marrett, and Mr. Sprague, of Carlisle, exchanged pulpits, and a fast was held on August 1.

This custom of exchanging pulpits and entertaining visiting clerics may have been in reaction to the period when pulpits had been denied to Whitefield because his sermons were disruptive. It was a symbol that churches were at peace with one another.

Apparently the drought of the early summer of 1776 was broken by heavy rainfall. On that occasion, Mr. Penniman implied he expected God to be reasonable:

> "We prayed, O Lord, for rain, but we did not wish
> Thou shouldst leave the bottles of Heaven unstopped."

And later he said,

> "We did ask, O Lord, that Thou wouldst uncork the
> bottles of Heaven, but we sought not Thou wouldst throw
> away the stoppers." [11]

Fig. 31. Molly Penniman's tombstone (1971 rubbing)

His unusual approach to God served him ill with Bedford's sober townsmen.

By 1778 the inflation caused by the war had decreased the value of Penniman's income. Joseph asked if the townsmen would grant him any sum of money in addition to his stated salary for one year. Moreover, he reported, the collector had given him £9 in bad money which had cost him 10s in interest. Would they make good the £9 and allow him 10s? They doubled his salary and gave him £9 10s. The next year he needed to ask them for another increase. They gave him £500 in addition to his basic salary, but in 1780 when the matter arose, they gave him fifty bushels of rye and fifty of Indian corn in place of currency. Joseph was content with the grain.

One of Joseph's brothers, Mesheck Penniman, who had recently married Ruth Dwelle, bought the home of Israel Putnam, the Deacon's son, and came there to live near Joseph. The townsmen voted not to tax Mesheck since he was part of a ministerial family.

Not long after Mesheck's marriage, tragedy came to Joseph and Hannah, when little Molly Penniman died. No one but Joseph could have designed the tombstone which marked her grave.

IN
Memory of Molly
Penniman Daughter of
Rev*d* Mr Joseph & M*rs*
Hannah Penniman
who departed this Life
August 21 1778 Aged 3
Years 6 Months & 3 Days
Ah dear Polly must your tender parents mourn
Their heavy loss & bathe with tears your urn
Since now no more to us you must return

It was not like any in the burying place. The epitaph was a rhymed triplet expressing only the grief of parents who had loved a little girl and playfully called her Polly. It contained no religious sentiment.

The townsmen considered it an example of Mr. Penniman's eccentricity, a quality they more and more frequently noted.

That same year, John Reed had the misfortune to lose one daughter, and two years later, another. Their epitaphs were likely what

John's neighbors expected to read. Both warned that even young people must be prepared for unexpected death, and one mentioned the pre-millennium which Jonathan Edwards had described:

Memento mori
In Memory of
Grace Reed Daught:
of John Reed Esqr:
and Mrs Ruhamah his
wife, who Died Sept
16th 1778, In the 19th
year of her Age.
From Deaths arrest no age is free,
As beholders may see, & Now dear
youth, Brothers, sisters, & friends all
Prepare to come for sure you must,
And mingle with me in ye Dust.

Memento mori
In memory of
Eliot Reed Daught:
of John Reed Esqr. &
Mrs Ruhamah his
wife who Died Augt
24th: 1780. In the 16th
year of her age.
How uncertain is this Life how
little did I expect to die so young
Dear youth Remember my sudden
Death for in such an hour as
ye think not ye son of man cometh

As soon as the battles of the Revolution had ended, the townsmen commenced the meetinghouse repairs which had been postponed for six years. They asked a committee to determine what materials were needed and what they would cost. Soon they knew that £1000 was necessary and they assessed the inhabitants accordingly. Reuben Duren, an architect and builder who had moved from Billerica to Bedford recently, was in charge of the work.

Mr. Duren was also building a new home for Lieutenant Timothy Jones, which was assembled and raised in sections as meetinghouses were. Mr. Penniman gave the prayer for the raising, and once again his prayer was considered odd and ill-advised. Some said he had taken too much of the mixed drink served at the occasion.

Later that day, as he rode to his home, it was said that he fell from his horse, losing his clerical wig. The wig was discovered by some boys who put it in a hollow log near Penniman's home. After some time the boys asked Joseph to help them catch a woodchuck which had scurried into the log. There was no woodchuck, but Joseph found his wig.

In the fall of 1781, Mr. Penniman took part in the ordination of Carlisle's first resident minister, Paul Litchfield. Previously the people had heard sermons from Mr. Sprague, who had supplied the pulpit.

Hannah Penniman's fourth daughter was born that season. She was Polly, the nickname the Penniman's had used for Molly.

The decreasing value of money was a burden on the townsmen, both for the necessary increases in the minister's salary and for meetinghouse repairs. They could not decide whether to pay Mr. Penniman in hard money or in paper, finally giving him fifty hard dollars because of the depreciation, and hoping he would sign a receipt in the clerk's book. They had to increase the repair tax by £180 because £1000 had not been enough to complete work on the meetinghouse. There was discussion and indecision; finally the voters requested that the accounts of both the ministerial salary and the repairs to the meetinghouse be kept apart from other town expenses. This was the first indication that the day might come when the entire cost of public worship would be paid from sources other than tax funds.

Still the repairs could not be completed. The timbers needed capping and the house was not painted. The townsmen shunned further responsibility, saying the committee in charge were to do what they thought best. It was clear they would spend no more on the old house.

Moreover, a group of townsmen, probably members of the church, were not satisfied with what had been done. They wanted the building modernized by adding a porch, a tower, or a steeple. New houses had been built with these features, and some old ones

courtesy the Concord Free Public Library

Fig. 32. Concord's meetinghouse, built in 1710-11, as remodeled in 1791-92 (photograph of a painting on wood)

were remodeled to include them. These townsmen placed an article in the warrant for town meeting on September 1, 1783, "to see if the town will . . . erect and build up adjoining to the meetinghouse a tower and steeple to hang the bell therein, or a porch or porches, or any or either of them . . ." [14]

At the meeting the majority voted against building any additions to the meetinghouse at town cost. However, townsmen agreed to make additions by building a tower, a steeple, and a porch adjacent to the meetinghouse without charge to the town.

In this way, they gave permission for the church to meet in a churchlike building provided they were not taxed for the cost.

By December the group wanting a remodeled house had found the core of the problem. They asked the townsmen to establish a method to receive money to repair the meetinghouse so that the town need not be taxed. The townsmen voted that pew ground should be sold to meet the expenses. For about thirty years after that, practically no tax money was used for a meetinghouse in Bedford, and the people depended on the sale of more and more pew ground as the source of necessary funds. As churchmen, they had no legal right to raise money or pay costs other than as the townsmen granted it to them. They were still the town's church.

Eight years later, some inhabitants of Concord wanted to remodel their meetinghouse. With Bedford as an example, they knew how to proceed. They had on hand some tax money allotted to the meetinghouse. Old pew owners promised to pay their share of the cost even though they would not need pew ground. Some additional pew ground would be available after the inside stairs were moved into the new porch, and some members of the congregation wanted to buy pew ground. With money from these three sources, they did extensive alterations, lowering the roof, adding a porch, tower and steeple. They, too, planned to be free of expense to the town. Their remodeled meetinghouse probably looked like the one Bedford's men had hoped to have. (Fig. 32)

In preparation for repairs in Bedford, a committee searched the records to see what pew ground the town owned and what could be sold. They questioned the titles of the pews used by David Fitch, Lieutenant Timothy Jones, Captain John Moore, and Israel Putnam, wondering whether the ground under them could be included in the sale.

David Fitch was the grandson of Samuel, who had no pew in the meetinghouse. David's father had bought Jonathan Bacon's home and mill on the Shawsheen River, but Jonathan had had no pew to include in the sale. David had his father's property and a pew. He himself did not know from whom it came. Nine years earlier he had asked the townsmen if he owned the pew he was improving, and they tabled his question. Now they found no evidence, pro or con.

Lieutenant Timothy Jones owned one part of Joseph Dean's land. Mr. Dean had been denied pew ground and would have had no pew to sell. The committee was unsuccessful in discovering how the Lieutenant got one. However, somewhat earlier, the Lieutenant had set a window in his pew with the town's permission. Since the corner pews under the gallery were dark, it is believed his window had been set into the north wall, lighting the pew which had been Joseph Bacon's.

Captain John Moore had another part of Joseph Dean's land. Mrs. Susanna Dean had bequeathed her "meetinghouse pue" to John Moore, the Captain's father, who had been killed when he was swept from a load of hay by the frame of a door as he was riding into the barn. The Captain had his father's pew, but no one knew from whom Susanna Dean had acquired it.

Israel Putnam, Jr., had sold his place to Mesheck Penniman and was living in Chelmsford near his brother Jonathan's family. Yet the committee inquired about his pew. His father, the Deacon, had been granted none, but his mother's estate had had a third of a pew. Her sons Israel and Benjamin shared her estate and a whole pew. Benjamin scarcely outlived his mother, so Israel and his family used the whole pew. The committee could not establish from whom the Deacon had purchased a third of a pew nor how the Putnams came to have the other two thirds.

The townsmen decided to relinquish any claim to the ground under these four pews.

The ground they were selling on the floor was under the town's remaining seats for its congregation. They took a strip 4½ inches wide out of the alley in front of the pulpit to add to the pew ground, while they widened the side alleys by planning the pews to be about a foot shorter than those in the south part of the house. They marked out eight lots, four on each side of the middle alley, five for sale and three to be kept by the town (two directly in front of the pulpit and one near the west door). (Fig. 33)

No longer was there a rule saying only one family could own a pew, but the vendue master sold each lot to one person. However, before the sale, prospective owners met in small neighborhoods to decide how each lot was to be subdivided, resulting in two or three persons owning a lot and using it with others of their choice. The final records were complicated.

William Hartwell's son Stephen had bought a pew lot in 1753 to help buy a bell, and now he bought one to repair the meeting-house, but he requested that it be recorded as belonging to Oliver Bacon and Jonas Gleason. Oliver lived on the east side of the Shawsheen River near Vine Brook. Jonas operated a mill on Vine Brook and was Oliver's neighbor.

Stephen Hartwell, Jr., bought a lot which was to be listed as the property of the brothers, William and David Page. Because David continued to wear Continental costumes and walked regally, his neighbors called him "King David."

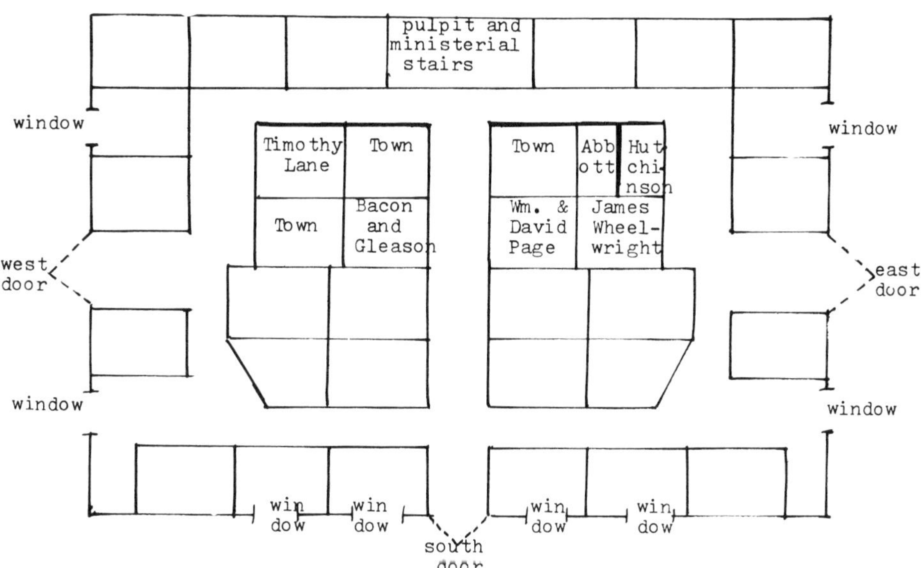

Fig. 33. Sale of pew ground * to raise money for repairs,
1784 (drawn from information in Bedford town records)
* Scale: 8 feet to 1 inch

Lieutenant Moses Abbott, or "Solid Abbott," as he was called, bought a lot, one half of which was written as belonging to his neighbor Benjamin Hutchinson.

Timothy Lane and a tanner listed, it is believed, in error as James Wheelwright, kept the titles to the lots they purchased. (James Wheelwright was probably James Wright, later to be named a deacon.)

There were two rows of lots across the south gallery, five in front and seven in back of an alley and against the wall. Six of these twelve were sold. Three in the center of the front row were bought by three men who gave them to the town for the use of the singers during public worship services. (Fig. 34)

John Reed, Esquire, financed one. He had earned his title by representing the town on the Committee of Inspection, the Committee of Correspondence, at the First and Second Provincial Congresses, at the Constitutional Convention for the Commonwealth of Massachusetts, and at the General Court.

James Lane gave money for a second singers' pew.

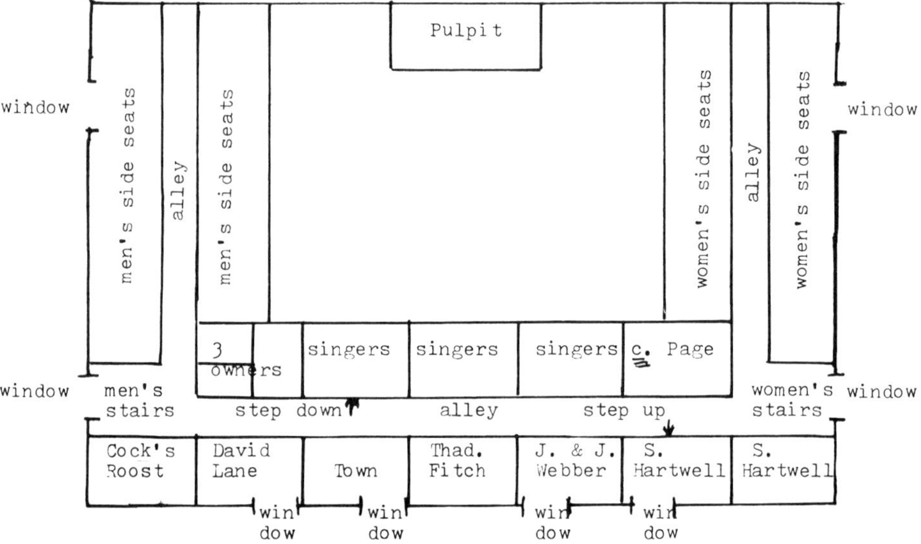

Fig. 34. Sale of pew ground in the gallery * to raise money
for repairs, 1784 (drawn from information in Bedford town
records)

* Scale: 8 feet to 1 inch

Nathaniel Page, cousin of William and David, contributed the money for the third lot for the singers. The total gift of these three came to $128.

Captain Christopher Page, a cousin of William, David, and Nathaniel, bought the lot to the east side of the singers.

Lieutenant Moses Abbott purchased the one on the west of the singers, keeping one quarter for his use and asking that Captain Edward Stearns, brother of the teacher-minister Josiah, be listed as the owner of one half and Lieutenant John Merriam as owner of the remaining quarter.

Stephen Hartwell and Stephen, Jr., bought two lots against the wall, returning their titles to the town to be resold, thus contributing $39.50. David Bacon gave $18.50 to the town, when he bought one of the Hartwell lots and requested that the town resell it. John Webber, husband of Susanna Fassett, and his son John, Jr., purchased it, while Thaddeus Fitch bought the second Hartwell lot and kept it for himself.

The total from the sale of the lots and the gifts was $727, or nearly £182. Now the committee in charge of repairs brought in a bill for $992, or £248 for the work already done, including setting glass over the doors, securing the galleries with four dogs,* capping the posts and girts,** and refinishing the pulpit. An additional $265, or £66 was needed to meet these costs. Some thought another public sale should be held, but it is likely that three lots were sold privately, one near the west door, and the two end lots in the wall row in the south gallery. Even so, it was four years before Reuben Duren was paid in full. The meetinghouse never had a porch, a tower, or a steeple.

Mr. Duren bought, perhaps from Stephen Hartwell, the wall pew in the southeast corner of the south gallery next to the women's stairs. It and its mate in the southwest corner were the "cock's roosts" or "cock loft." Mr. Duren owned this even after he moved back to Billerica, at last selling it to Captain William Goodrich (or Goodridge), of Bedford. The town clerk made a record of the sale "a pew . . . called the cock's roost." The Reverend Dr. William A.

---

* Devices for holding, gripping, or fastening something; a rod, hook, or claw.
** Timbers used as footing for the roof rafters.

Stearns remembered these seats from his boyhood. ". . . Up back," he said, "high in the corners, or cock loft, as they called it, were the negro pews, rarely occupied by more than one or two of that class of worshippers."[15]

The townsmen voted to shut the east and west doors in the winter season when it was very windy or stormy. To assist the singers, who sat in the front gallery next to the men's side seats, they named two new music leaders.

During that autumn (1784) Joseph Penniman became too ill to preach, and by the first of December, the townsmen appointed a committee to provide preaching for a month, hoping Mr. Penniman would have recovered by the new year.

In 1786 a committee was named to paint the meetinghouse. The clapboard siding was five years old, and Lieutenant Timothy Jones's odd window was in place, possibly in the north wall. The committee-men selected the color; it was "Bedford Yellow," and probably the only paint the building ever had.* William Stearns said it had been shabby in his youth, covered with a thin coat of dirty yellow. He was speaking of a time some thirty years after the "Bedford Yellow" had been applied.

Another committee set the bellhouse "square," shortened its steeple, and turned the bell around, suggesting that one side was cracked. Annually for ten years they inspected it to see if it could still be used, and finally put it in storage, from which it was later sold.

Deacon Stephen Davis retired at sixty-nine, and James Wright was named to replace him. James had been a singing leader when Watts's Version was introduced, and he had served as special town treasurer when the pew lots had been sold. Later he was to be listed as owning a pew near the east door, suggesting the rule seating the deacons east of the pulpit was abandoned, or that he was al-lowed to have a pew for his family if he wished.

Deacon Davis died two years later. Identical tombstones were erected for him and his wife. Upon the death of his daughter-in-law, a similar stone would mark her grave.

---

* A locally produced yellow ochre used as a pigment or stain.

In Memory of
Deacon Stephen Davis,
who died
July ye 22d AD 1787;
Aged 71 years
and 8 months
The sweet remembrance of ye just,
Shall florish when they sleep in dust.

In Memory of
Mrs: Elizabeth Davis
(Relict of
Deacon Stephen Davis)
who died
Decr: ye 5th: AD. 1789;
Aged 71 years &
3 months
Bless'd are the dead, yea saith the word,
That die in Christ the living Lord.

In Memory of
Mrs. Sarah Davis,
wife of
Dean Thaddeus Davis,
who died May 26, 1807,
Aged 47 years 9 M. & 23 D.
The grave of all the saints he bles'd
And soften'd every bed
Where should the dying members rest
But with the dying head.*

On them, dust had been remembered and salvation as unity with Christ had been declared.

When Deacon Benjamin Bacon died, the church named no one to his office for five years. Both his son Elijah and his wife had preceded him, and all the epitaphs were the simple memorials of an earlier day:

---

* Members of the church were saints who would rest with Christ, the head of the Church, Christ who died for them. These words are the 4th verse of Watts's burial hymn, "Why do we mourn departed friends?"

Sacred
to the Memory of
Deacon Benjamin Bacon
who departed this Life
October 1st 1791
Aet 78.
Go—Traviler live to God.

In Memory of
Mrs Katharine Bacon
wife of
Deacon Benjamin Bacon
who died July 17th
1791
aged 74 years.

In Memory of
Mr. Elijah Bacon
who departed this Life
Septr 13th, 1788
Aged 34 years.

The deacon had one surviving son, who lost his wife somewhat later. In her epitaph, without resting in the dust or the tomb, without hearing the trumpet, she went to a pleasant place to meet pleasant people:

In Memory of
Mrs Amittai Bacon
wife of
Mr. Benjamin Bacon
who died
Octr. 10, 1806;
Aged 48.
Farewell kind friends a short farewell
Till we shall meet again above
In paradise, where pleasures dwell;
And kindred souls rejoice in love

After being near Joseph for about ten years, Mesheck and Ruth Penniman moved away. Joseph bought their property, selling it to James Lane the third in a year or so. Joseph had bought seventeen acres from Israel Putnam, Jr., when Mesheck had purchased his home. Now Joseph had Reuben Duren build him a new home on that land. It was to be more distinguished than Pollard's inn, and Mr. Duren designed it with balance and charm. (Fig. 35)

While the new house was going up, Prisca was born to the Pennimans. Her name is an ancient spelling of Priscilla. Now there were four daughters to move with Joseph and Hannah.

They had been in the new house two years when they were again stricken by the death of their oldest child. In the first four lines that Joseph wrote for Hannah's tombstone, he spoke to his daughter, knowing she could not reply. Then he broke the rhythm of his verse by alluding to Judgment Day. He kept the last three lines together and apart with a bracket. They described Hannah's resurrection and seem to have been written to please his church and congregation, to silence their criticism, to show that he respected their beliefs. He may have written first what he felt and then broken the rhythm to write what his people thought was fitting. (Fig. 36)

Hannah Penniman
Daughter of the Revd
Joseph Penniman and
Hannah Penniman depar-
ted this Life Dec 22d 1790
aged 18 years 4 months
& 11 days

Ah! now, No notice do you give,
Where you are how you live:
What! are you then bound by Solemn
To keep the secret of your state; (fate
The alarming Voice you will hear
When Christ the judge shall appear

Hannah! from this dark lonely Vault
Certainly soon & suddenly you'll come
When Jesus shall claim the Treasure
from the Tomb.

Fig. 35. The Penniman-Stearns house

Fig. 36. Hannah Penniman's tombstone (from a 1971 rubbing)

In the meetinghouse, the singers' benches were probably as old as the gallery itself. They needed repair, and the townsmen took the women's side seats in the side gallery for the use of the singers. The action was a kind of eminent domain. Even these seats needed attention, for the voters decided to "let them be made convenient for them to sit in without damaging them."* [16] With this permission, the singers moved from the south to the east gallery.

As part of his duties, Mr. Penniman visited the school, praying before he left. The children must have repeated one of his prayers to their parents, for it became one of the stock anecdotes about Joseph's eccentricity:

> "We pray thee, O Lord, that these children may be
> well trained at home, for if they are not, they will act like
> Sarpints when they are abroad." [17]

Joseph administered the church under the covenant which allowed baptized and regenerate persons to be members, whether or not they observed the Lord's supper. If this covenant was intended to increase the membership, it failed after the first flurry, for the rate of growth declined to two new members a year. If the covenant was intended to encourage baptism of children, it succeeded, for Joseph performed that ordinance nine times a year, or almost two hundred times during his ministry. That was in Bedford, but he also conducted the ceremony in other places. Ebenezer Bridge, of Chelmsford, who as a young man had ridden to Bedford to attend the burial of Nicholas Bowes, died in 1792. During the time that church was without a leader, Joseph Penniman, Ezra Ripley, of Concord, and Henry Cumings, of Billerica, served in the pulpit.

Joseph may have pleased Chelmsford Church, but on the first Sabbath in July 1793, he displeased Bedford's. It was Communion Day, and he did something which "grieved" the members; that is, they were sorrowful and troubled.

Five days later, the members met at the home of Deacon James Wright, on the north side of the road from the meetinghouse to Woburn and Lexington. They recorded their discussion, generalizing their complaint and concealing the cause of their distress. They "held a conference with each other respecting the unchristianlike

---

* Did the singers do damage to the seats, or the seats to the singers?

behavior of their Pastor, Mr. Joseph Penniman, the last Lord's day, it being communion day, and every member of said church being grieved thereat." [18]

Members of the church were concerned with personal religious experiences, intimacies between themselves and God. They expressed their concern in singing and reading, in worship services and prayer, and in ordinances. Anything they considered disrespectful to their expressions of concern would be "unchristianlike," or not like a redeemed man. So Mr. Penniman had behaved like an unregenerate person at communion. One hundred years later (1891) Abram English Brown in *History of Bedford* defined "unchristianlike" differently, saying, "In the light of the present, it would be declared that strong drink caused the trouble." [19]

The church was so disturbed that it closed the doors of the meetinghouse to its minister. This act brought Bedford into disfavor in the neighboring towns. After two months, churchmen asked townsmen if they would "have the church refer their grievances in respect to the Reverend Mr. Joseph Penniman to a council, provided Mr. Penniman doth not agree to have the relation in which he stands to the church and the town dissolved?"[20] The townsmen said yes, a council meeting should be held. They asked Moses Fitch and Thompson Bacon to work with the church's committee in presenting the case to the council and three others to provide food and lodging for the council members.

The meeting was held at the end of October 1793. Those who came were Josiah Bridge, of East Sudbury (now Wayland); Henry Cumings, of Billerica; Jacob Cushing, of Waltham; Samuel Kendal, of Weston; Jedidiah Morse, of Charlestown, and Phillips Payson, of Chelsea (now Revere). They sat three days, and the town paid £33 for their entertainment.

All these men were remarkable for their integrity and leadership, their understanding, and their contribution to the culture in which they lived.[21]

Josiah Bridge, a Harvard graduate, son of Deacon John and Sarah Bridge, of Lexington, had preached in East Sudbury for thirty-six years. His work has been evaluated as that of an Arminian, perhaps because he believed a minister should read, pray, meditate, set an example for others in his own life, and serve everyone in his flock. But he also demonstrated a thoughtful transition between the emotional enthusiasm of an earlier day and the erudition of the ministry twenty-five or thirty years later. Mr. Bridge believed man had both temporal and physical components and spiritual qualities. To improve the spiritual, ministers should build their churches on the prophets and apostles, the doctrine of the Gospel, not on the commandments of men (probably not on the sermons of Whitefield and others). Inspired by the Holy Ghost, ministers should teach the discipline of Christ and the meaning of the crucifixion.

Mr. Bridge had a pleasant voice and sound judgment based on scientific and theological knowledge. His advice as peacemaker was honored, and those who knew him esteemed him.

Henry Cumings had had Billerica's pulpit for thirty-six years. He had taken as his second wife Sarah, daughter of Ebenezer Bridge, of Chelmsford. He avoided "ensnaring and delusive sophistry of unprincipled libertines," the "wild vagaries of blind enthusiasm, baneful influence of unenlightened party zeal." [22] He was an Arminian.

Jacob Cushing was the son of the Reverend Job and Mary Cushing. As a Harvard graduate, he had been ordained in Waltham before Nicholas Bowes had been dismissed in Bedford, and John Hancock had given him his charge. He had married Anna, daughter of one of Bowes's friends, Warham Williams of Waltham. During Mr. Cushing's ministry, he admitted 369 members to his church and he baptized 1,736. He believed the purpose of Christianity was to restore mankind to an offended Maker. It was a perfect institution for this purpose, revealing as it did the love, grace, peace, and goodwill which came from God. The church needed no extraordinary personnel for its mission, no one preaching doctrines or rules of life. "Those who, in this age, pretend they have an immediate revelation from heaven to preach the gospel are to be considered as seducers and treated with deserved contempt."[23] He did believe knowledge of God was experimental and transforming; the good works which resulted were to be based on natural powers and abilities. These talents were to be developed through broad education and aquisition of wisdom. Like Josiah Bridge, he represented a transitional period between emotionalism and insight.

Samuel Kendal was, through marriage, Mrs. Jacob Cushing's nephew. He had preached in Weston about ten years, ever since his graduation from Harvard College. He followed his father-in-law, Samuel Woodward, who had ministered there thirty-one years. Mr.

Woodward had avoided extremes and did not deal with controversies. He believed in mending the lives of those he touched, and that man's moral improvement was his happiness. Mr. Kendal extended this kindly pastorate until he died in 1814. He preached the great truths of Christ, free of dogmas, sect, and party. His work has been evaluated as Arminian.

Jedidiah Morse was an orthodox Calvinist. Born in Connecticut, he had been graduated from Yale College and had married the granddaughter of Samuel Finley, a Presbyterian minister and President of the College of New Jersey (now Princeton). He was thirty and new to Charlestown, but he was to work there for thirty years. He was a tall man with bright eyes and silken hair which he wore powdered and curled. He was a sensitive intellectual. He helped create Andover Theological Seminary, where the concepts of salvation and justification were taught, and Park Street Church in Boston, which practiced a strict form of Calvinism. With a full program of ministerial and theological work, he was a physical scientist who wrote a series of textbooks on American Geography which had many editions and are available today among old, rare books. (Fig. 37) He became known as the father of American Geography. His son was Samuel F. B. Morse.

Phillips Payson, son of the Reverend Phillip and Ann Payson, of Walpole, had preached in Chelsea for forty years. He had three relatives in the ministry: his brother Seth was at Rindge, New Hampshire; his brother John was at Fitchburg, Massachusetts; and Samuel, probably a cousin, was at Lunenburg, Massachusetts. Phillips's pulpit had been Thomas Cheever's, a pulpit from which Whitefield had preached and served communion in 1744. Phillips's method of preaching and performing his pastoral duties was Calvinistic, but he had spoken beyond the usual definition of Calvinism when he told his brother Seth that we should unite in charity and love, although we are of different opinions. He had reminded Samuel that the Gospel message should be delivered free from human errors. Phillips Payson was the minister who had aided in the capture of twelve British soldiers while Joseph Penniman prayed.

Six religious leaders comprised the council in Bedford, two Arminians, two Calvinists, and two who represented a transitional period in religious thought. An enrichment had come about when those ideas of both the Old and the New Lights which were not in

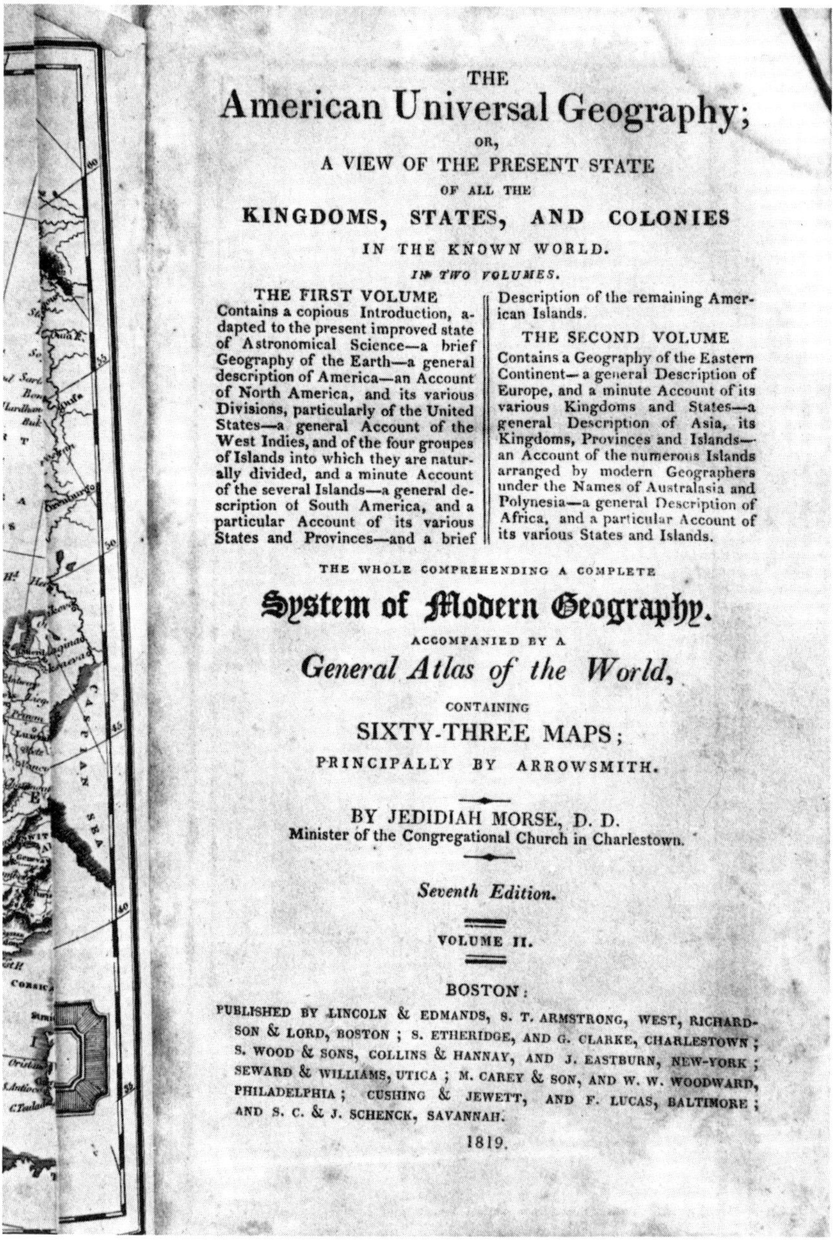

THE

American Universal Geography;

OR,

A VIEW OF THE PRESENT STATE

OF ALL THE

KINGDOMS, STATES, AND COLONIES

IN THE KNOWN WORLD.

IN TWO VOLUMES.

THE FIRST VOLUME
Contains a copious Introduction, a-dapted to the present improved state of Astronomical Science—a brief Geography of the Earth—a general description of America—an Account of North America, and its various Divisions, particularly of the United States—a general Account of the West Indies, and of the four groupes of Islands into which they are natur-ally divided, and a minute Account of the several Islands—a general de-scription of South America, and a particular Account of its various States and Provinces—and a brief

Description of the remaining Amer-ican Islands.

THE SECOND VOLUME
Contains a Geography of the Eastern Continent— a general Description of Europe, and a minute Account of its various Kingdoms and States—a general Description of Asia, its Kingdoms, Provinces and Islands—an Account of the numerous Islands arranged by modern Geographers under the Names of Australasia and Polynesia—a general Description of Africa, and a particular Account of its various States and Islands.

THE WHOLE COMPREHENDING A COMPLETE

System of Modern Geography.

ACCOMPANIED BY A

General Atlas of the World,

CONTAINING

SIXTY-THREE MAPS;

PRINCIPALLY BY ARROWSMITH.

BY JEDIDIAH MORSE, D. D.

Minister of the Congregational Church in Charlestown.

Seventh Edition.

VOLUME II.

BOSTON:

PUBLISHED BY LINCOLN & EDMANDS, S. T. ARMSTRONG, WEST, RICHARD-SON & LORD, BOSTON ; S. ETHERIDGE, AND G. CLARKE, CHARLESTOWN ; S. WOOD & SONS, COLLINS & HANNAY, AND J. EASTBURN, NEW-YORK ; SEWARD & WILLIAMS, UTICA ; M. CAREY & SON, AND W. W. WOODWARD, PHILADELPHIA ; CUSHING & JEWETT, AND F. LUCAS, BALTIMORE ; AND S. C. & J. SCHENCK, SAVANNAH.

1819.

Fig. 37. Title page of an edition of the Reverend Jedidiah
Morse's *Geography* (1972 photograph)

contradiction had been mixed and expanded by adding graciousness. The change was shown in the life of a minister named Ezra Stiles.

Ezra was the son of a Congregational minister, becoming a member of his father's church at nineteen. But he spent the next seven years in uncertainty and soul-searching. At last he took a journey through the northeastern provinces, visiting churches of Quakers, Dutch Calvinists, Roman Catholics, Episcopalians, and Congregationalists. He learned that each group had its own approach to religion, and it was unprofitable to expect a change. He preferred the scriptural model of Congregationalism. He entered the ministry in Newport, Rhode Island, where he became a friend of Rabbi Isaac Carigal. He gave a "Discourse on the Christian Union" before a convention of Congregational ministers in Bristol, Rhode Island. He said there could be no restriction on conscience, for its right was inalienable. In order to build toward the future, one must inquire where the Old and New Light agreed, examine their beliefs with scripture as a reference, walk together as far as possible, forbear differences in love, and remember that all have their private judgment in religion.

This was in 1760, and by 1793 when the council met in Bedford, many ministers were following the path of Stiles. The council sat for three days, at last recommending that there be a separation between Mr. Penniman and the church and town.

The church agreed, and on November 25 the townsmen concurred, saying they would exempt Mr. Joseph Penniman's estate from taxation, provided he continued to live in the town and occupy the same property so long under his improvement. They granted £70 for extraordinary costs because of the changed circumstances, and named a committee to supply the pulpit.

Someone tacked a piece of doggerel on one of the meetinghouse doors:

> "A wicked priest, a crooked people,
> A cracked bell without a steeple."[24]

It was a "pox on both your houses"

It is probable that the people just did not understand Joseph Penniman, his lively imagination, his sense of humor, and his inclination to verse. Ever since the day when he had lost his wig near Lieutenant Timothy Jones's house, they had believed he drank too much. Joseph was fifty-six. He did not resign from the office of

Fig. 38. The home of Reverend Mr. Joseph Penniman in
Harvard, Massachusetts

minister. He moved his family to the town of Harvard, buying a seventy-year-old house from Eleazer Hamlin. It still stands on the road from Harvard to Ayer, about two miles from the center of town.[25] (Fig. 38)

In Harvard the townsmen had voted a sum of money to pay their minister and to support and maintain other teachers of piety, religion, and morality. Joseph assisted the resident Congregational minister of Harvard, William Emerson.

Soon he became known for his images and fancies, his "quaint conceits." He continued to talk to God as if He were a neighbor. When drought was a problem, he asked God to "vouchsafe that the bottles of heaven may be uncocked and their refreshing waters poured upon the parched fields." Canker worms were a serious pest, destroying foliage on many kinds of plants. Joseph was dismayed when they invaded orchards:

> "We pray, O Lord, that thou wilt take pity upon us
> and remove from our midst these voracious canker worms,
> for if thou lookest over this town, thou wilt see that every
> apple tree is as red as a fox's tail." [26]

During an epidemic, Joseph visited a family having three ill persons. Trying to please all three, he stood at the head of the stairs where he could be heard by all of them, and prayed:

> "Be very merciful unto Bezaleel who lieth nigh unto
> death in the north chamber . . . Send thy ministering
> angels to comfort Bathsheba, groaning with anguish in the
> south chamber . . . visit with thy healing grace Judith,
> thy sorely afflicted hand maiden, in the bedroom down
> stairs." [27]

Joseph helped William Emerson only a few years before Mr. Emerson moved to the pulpit in the First Church of Boston. There he was known as a Unitarian. His son, Ralph Waldo Emerson, was born while he had that pulpit.

In Harvard, Mr. Emerson is remembered as a Universalist. It is probable that he and Joseph had an agreement before Joseph moved to Harvard. In that case, Joseph too would have been considered a Universalist by his colleagues. There is no rumor in Harvard that he took too many intoxicants.

In 1804, Joseph's daughter Lucy married a townsman of Harvard, Zaccheus Gates, son of Captain Isaac and Submit Gates. Four years later, Joseph Penniman died on August 30, 1808, at the age of seventy-one. It is possible that his grave was not marked, for it has not yet been discovered.

V

Fig. 39. The Reverend Mr. Samuel Stearns (reproduced from Abram English Brown, *History of the Town of Bedford*)

❧ THE REVEREND MR. SAMUEL STEARNS ☙

Ten days after Bedford dismissed Joseph Penniman, the church called an all-day fast. The members probably were seeking forgiveness for seeming to be a "crooked people," for they had no candidate in mind. The church was without a minister for two and a half years. Names of the interim supplies are not known, but the town spent £180 to pay them.

Solomon Lane, son of James and Mary (Wellington) Lane, was on the pulpit committee when a candidate was found. Solomon had clung to his family's tradition that the best wives came from ministerial households and had married Sarah Stearns, daughter of the Reverend Josiah and half-sister of the candidate, Samuel Stearns.[1] If Mary Lane had been influential in settling her cousins, Josiah and Nathaniel Sherman, perhaps Solomon's wife used her influence in behalf of her half-brother Samuel. (Fig. 39)

Samuel Stearns, twenty-five, was the firstborn of Josiah and his second wife, Sarah, daughter of the Reverend Samuel Ruggles, of Billerica. Samuel's early years had not been easy ones. Although his father had been the minister in Epping, New Hampshire, for thirty years, he had not been able to finance Samuel's college training. He had six daughters and five other sons for whom to provide and his ministry spanned the years of hardship following the Revolution. He had augmented his salary, however, with the produce from a small farm, and it had been necessary for Samuel to work in the fields as soon as he was old enough to be helpful. Josiah had died when Samuel was eighteen.

While doing an errand, Samuel met almost accidentally John Phillips, founder of Exeter Academy in New Hampshire. Mr. Phillips saw him as a lad with promising ability and offered on two occasions to help him prepare for college. Samuel had to refuse the first offer, but after his father's death and with his mother's encouragement, he accepted the second proposal. He studied at Exeter Academy during one year and enrolled at Dartmouth College for two years. On a visit to his home he hold his mother about his religious experience. She was so moved that she cried and at that time Samuel began to conduct the family prayers.

Before entering a third year at Dartmouth, Samuel consulted Mr. Phillips about transferring to Harvard College, a school nearer his home and one he believed offered more advantages. Actually Mr. Phillips did not like either school. He felt Dartmouth taught a variation of Calvinism wherein Adam's sin was not inherited by his descendants, and to him Harvard was a fountain of Arminianism, spreading the tenet that anyone seeking God's grace would receive it. However, he did not oppose Samuel's transfer.

While Samuel was at Harvard, disorders among students were so prevalent that serious scholars were aggravated into intolerance. Samuel joined with a group ironically called the "Judas Club" to sign a statement saying they would expose anyone they caught rioting and causing destruction. The statement was read before prayers and as a result Samuel and his roommates were besieged by a student leading some drunken sailors. The roommates armed themselves with clubs and stood behind their locked door, expecting it to be broken in, but the door was strong and it withstood the attack. The attention of those outside was diverted and they fell away, struggling with each other. No one was hurt, and the roommates did reveal the name of the student, for he was expelled.

After graduating in 1794, Samuel administered an academy for boys in Andover, Massachusetts, which had been organized sixteen years before by John Phillips's nephew. The minister of Andover, Jonathan French, was a trustee of the academy. He was a cheerful, friendly man, a friend of the Phillips family, and he kept open house for divinity students. Samuel read theology with him.

Mr. French was a sensitive man, a Calvinist who disliked controversy. If he was excited, he retreated into his study and did not emerge until he was serene. One of his colleagues said, "He was reputed a Calvinist, though living in the atmosphere of Arminianism."[2] He was the father of three children, two daughters and a son. Samuel Stearns had fallen in love with the oldest, Abigail, eighteen, by the time a letter arrived, offering him Bedford's pulpit.

He had always known Bedford. His father had been respected there, when as a young man he had supplied the pulpit several times between Mr. Bowes's and Mr. Sherman's ministries. In addition, Samuel had two large families of cousins in Bedford and in the neighboring part of Billerica. They, too, were young adults, but nine of them had settled near their parents. Probably Samuel knew the reason for Mr. Penniman's dismissal and understood the varying religious opinions in the church, the congregation, and the town. However, he may have considered it a difficult pulpit, or even that it was entertaining Arminianism because, regardless of the homes where he was welcome, he wrote a letter of regret, refusing the offer.

Before he had sealed the letter, several people from Bedford called on him, asking him to delay his answer for a week. Who the callers were is not known, but they were effective in causing Samuel to change his mind. He destroyed the letter and wrote another, accepting the pulpit in Bedford.*

The town offered him a choice for salary. He could select either $333.33 and 3 mills with twenty cords of wood, or the same value in food with eighteen cords of wood. If he chose the food, he would receive the value of $83.33 and 3 mills in each of four kinds:

> Indian corn at 6¢ and 6 mills/bushel
> rye   at 83¢ and 3 mills/bushel
> beef   at $4.16 and 6 1/3 mills/hundredweight
> and pork   at 5¢ and 5 mills/pound

At these prices his salary would be 125 bushels of Indian corn, 100 bushels of rye, 2,000 pounds of beef, 1,515.5 pounds of pork, and eighteen cords of wood. In either case his settlement fee was $850.

Mr. Stearns replied that he preferred the food for several reasons, the instability of currency, the fair distribution of agricultural labor among the townsmen, and so on, but he believed some of the

---

* Samuel's signature as traced from the town clerk's record book in Bedford:

Samuel Stearns.

townsmen were opposed to payment in food. For the sake of peace and harmony, he would accept currency, trusting the townsmen to protect him in case of its depreciation. And he asked for an annual vacation of two Sabbaths in a year to visit distant friends.

The townsmen approved and named Wednesday, April 25, 1796, as the day for the ordination. Colonel Timothy Jones offered to entertain the visiting council in his home.

Committees were appointed to prepare the meetinghouse, inside and out, for the event. The galleries were propped up, four pews in front of the pulpit and those on either end of it were reserved for the guests, and five seats in the gallery were kept for the singers. The cracked bell was stored, the bellhouse sold at vendue, and the ground south of the house leveled. Booths were set up around the building where food and other items were to be sold to help support the church free of cost to the town.

The council was large, reflecting the desire of the church to be one of a community of churches, as it had been when Mr. Penniman had been ordained.

The ministers, Jonas Clark, of Lexington; Henry Cumings, of Billerica; John Marrett, of Burlington; Ezra Ripley, of Concord; and Paul Litchfield, of Carlisle, who had conducted the fast-day service two years previously, returned for the ordination. They were joined by Charles Stearns, of Lincoln (no relation); Mr. Alden, of Chelmsford; Dr. Joseph Willard, President of Harvard College; Dr. David Tappan, Hollis Professor of Divinity at the College; Jonathan French, of Andover; and the minister of Epping, New Hampshire. Deacons and messengers may have accompanied the clerics.

The ordination took place in the morning and the meetinghouse was full early. Charles Stearns gave the opening prayer. Jonathan French preached from Isa. 49:5: "Though Israel be not gathered, yet shall I be glorious in the eyes of the Lord, and my God shall be my strength." This seemed to say the church in Bedford was not gathered into the form of Calvinism Samuel Stearns exemplified, yet his work would be successful, and it was proven to be prophetic. John Marrett gave the ordaining prayer, Jonas Clark the charge, and Henry Cumings the right hand of fellowship. Mr. French spoke of the warmth between the people of Bedford and Samuel Stearns's father, regretting that he had not lived to see this day. Dr. Tappan gave the closing prayer.

The council left to dine with Colonel and Mrs. Jones, and neighboring townsmen laughingly accused the Bedford people of calling their minister before he left college, and settling him before he began to preach. Probably Samuel had been a frequent pulpit supply when he was studying.

With the pulpit filled, the church named William Merriam, grandson of Deacon Nathaniel Merriam and brother of Lydia Sherman, to the vacant deacon's seat. William had been groomed for this position by being asked to serve on committees for the church and town.

Samuel bought from Joseph Penniman the house Reuben Duren had built and brought his mother and two unmarried sisters, Mary and Elizabeth, to live with him there. He was methodical, and from the first practiced a routine. He spent enough time in his study to prepare two sermons for the Sabbath, often developing them into a series on a single subject. He did not expect them to be great, but earnest and clear, for he hoped to excite his people, teach them to be penitent, and encourage them to appeal to Christ for their salvation.

He believed I Tim. 4:16: ". . . in doing this, thou shalt both save thyself, and them that hear thee." On Sabbaths, he received written requests for help, often naming persons who were ill, and he reserved Mondays for visiting the sick. To them he was solicitous and comforting. "By faithful counsels . . . fervent prayers, tenderness, and concern, [a minister] manifests to the . . . sufferer how much he feels for the salvation of his soul." [3]

In May of 1797, Thursday the fourth was fast day, the Sabbath was the seventh, Monday was visiting day, and Tuesday, the ninth, was Samuel Stearns's wedding day. Abigail French was almost twenty-one. That very day Deacon James Wright called, bringing a cheese, three pounds of butter, three fowl, and sundries. Mr. Fassett came with a bushel of rye and a cheese. Nathaniel Page paid respect, leaving a bushel of rye and a bushel of potatoes. Colonel Jones brought four fowl. In this way, Abigail was welcomed to Bedford.

During the second year of his ministry, Mr. Stearns and the church rewrote the church covenant. The townsmen seemed unconcerned, for there was no public response. The new covenant was in two parts, the first being a substitute for the old Covenant of Grace.

In it, a candidate for membership begged his sins be forgiven, gave himself into everlasting covenant through the Redeemer, and promised to walk well like a saint. The second part dealt with the church and the candidate's relation to it.

It was no longer an agreement binding a group of people together in responsibility for the care of an institution, as the first covenant with Nicholas Bowes had been. Rather it was an understanding that each person who entered would be a member of a particular organization which was in Bedford. He would watch over and help other members, submitting to the power and discipline which the church had, and attending the ordinances and penalties which the church directed. Emphasis was placed on the ability of the individual, through his personal holiness, to maintain his relation to the institution, a tie he must daily pray that he could keep. Here was a group of people demonstrating the philosophy of Whitefield, for now there was no covenant between the members and God, but rather a delicate and indirect relationship through the mediation and judgment of Christ.

The new covenant's prologue was a "Confession of Faith." The prospective member professed to believe in God as a Trinity, in the fall and depravity of man, and in redemption through the intercession of Christ. He was convinced of the future existence of the soul, the resurrection of the body, a day of judgment, and a reward for good works.

The minister was to continue examining the candidates for membership, but Samuel Stearns rejected no one for weak faith if he showed hopeful signs of piety. When a new member was admitted to the church, the prologue and covenant were read aloud as the service of his election.

With the new covenant, Bedford's church had reached a goal. It had become a denomination, and it continued to believe in its perfection for some thirty years. Later it would use the words Orthodox Calvinist, or Trinitarian, to describe its philosophy. It continued to be a congregational church because its members directed its internal or religious affairs. However, depending in part on general tax funds as it did, it was to encounter difficult times. Yet they were far away.

During their first year in Bedford, the minister's family received many gifts, supplementing Samuel's salary, and he kept a list of them:

5 quantities of apples
1 pot of applesauce
1 leg of bacon
1 bushel of beets
118 ¾ pounds of beef
2 quarts of brandy
66½ pounds of butter
56 cabbages
1 calf's harslet, meat for a
  spit
38 candles
10½ cheeses
4 barrels of cider
3 cod fish
4½ bushels of Indian corn
2 dozen eggs
10 fowl
3 geese
3¼ lambs
1 leg of lamb
1 loin of lamb
½ bushel of onions
28 pigeons
3 pigs

1 hand of pork
2 legs of pork
193 pounds of pork
¼ of pork
3 spare ribs of pork
1 bag of potatoes
1 rake
1 bushel of rye
1 salmon
4 quantities of sauce: pickled
  roots, herbs, or salads
12 sausages
1 loaf of sugar
6 pounds of tallow
1 turkey
44 pounds of veal
1 leg of veal
1 loin of veal
1 barrel of vinegar
1 day's work with a cart
1 day's work with a plow
1½ day's work with a man
2 days' work with oxen[4]

In 1798 Abigail gave birth to her first child, a girl, who did not live. Before her second child, a girl they named for her mother, was born, George Washington had died. The Stearns family grew with the births of Samuel Horatio, named for his father, and Sarah Caroline, who had the name of both her grandmother Stearns and her aunt Sarah Lane.

The townsmen held a commemorative service for General Washington in the meetinghouse on February 22, 1800. Those who attended wore crepe on the left arm, and Colonel Timothy Jones, Cornet John Webber, Captain David Reed, and the two deacons opened the doors for the ceremony. Some people contributed to a fund of $26.40 to buy a piece of silk, probably a drape for the pulpit, which was given later to Mr. Stearns for his work in delivering a prayer and a dispensation. The twenty-second fell on a Friday, a day not included in the usual meaning of Samuel's contract.

Mr. Stearns asked the townsmen to revise the funeral customs followed in Bedford, which he considered to be in questionable taste. A funeral was not an ordinance and therefore not a church rite, nor had it been a legality, but a custom. The planters of the Colony believed a bell should toll and a company of neighbors should carry the dead to his grave, standing by during the burial. They agreed that "All prayers, either over or for the dead are not only superstitious and vain, but are also idolatry, and against the plain Scriptures of God." [5] The first change had come when the mourning family gave tokens of remembrance to the bearers and clerics who walked with them. John Hancock had received a ring at the burial of a minister in Woburn. [6] Gloves were an acceptable gift, and perhaps scarves. By 1800, at least in Bedford, the gift had changed once more to an offering of mixed drink, probably rum punch, which was passed around in pails, and Mr. Stearns objected.

After study, the townsmen established rules for funeral procedures and named a committee to advise the bereaved and to oversee the ceremony. Bearers were to be given advance notice of the time they were to serve. They were not to call on the mourners after the burial and no drinks were to be served, but prayers were to be attended one hour after the burial commenced. Probably the prayers were to be offered in the meetinghouse. Funerals in this manner were moved into the sphere of the church where they had not been until this time in New England.

Mr. Stearns had a tenor voice, and it is probable that he suggested the formation of a singing school, for the townsmen voted $20 toward its original expense and it continued for about twenty-five years. They also allowed Mr. Stearns's neighbor, Jeremiah Fitch, to put a window in his pew in the northwest corner of the meetinghouse. If Lieutenant Timothy Jones's window were in the northeast corner, symmetry was restored to the building. Many meetinghouses of this period had windows on four sides, and the necessity of setting two windows privately indicates Bedford's house was unusual.

The Stearns's second son, William Augustus, was born on Sunday, March 17, 1805. Although all the other children were baptized during the first week, William was baptized on the day of his birth. He was named for Samuel's brother, a deacon in the church in Epping where Josiah had preached. William's birth was followed by that of Maria H., Jonathan French, and Elizabeth W.

When he had worked in Bedford about six years, Samuel asked the townsmen to consider his embarassed circumstances resulting from the depreciation of the currency and to grant him some relief in any way they thought best. After two weeks of deliberation, the townsmen gave him the foods he had been offered earlier and voted to loan him the sum of $1,000 without interest during the time he held his ministry. He was to give the town sufficient security for the payment of the principal when he ceased preaching. To this, Mr. Stearns agreed.

Samuel and Abigail had much company. Ministers traveling through Bedford stopped at the Stearns's house as if it were a tavern. Their families sometimes rode with them, and often they were unexpected. They were always welcomed, fed, and lodged. Once Abigail prepared food for fourteen as well as for the nine or more in her own family in a twenty-four-hour period.

As his family grew, Samuel became more methodical, requiring household chores from the older children and supervising their religious training while they memorized the shorter catechism and passages from the Bible. A day began with morning prayers and a reading by one of the children from the Old Testament. It closed with evening prayers and a reading by the father from the New Testament. On Saturday, Samuel set his clock by a meridian in his doorway and opened the Sabbath shortly after tea by holding family devotions. Someone read from the Scriptures and Mr. Stearns prayed for his children, his church, his townsmen, and Harvard College where Arminianism flourished. From eight o'clock to nine o'clock he kept private devotions in his study, concentrating on a single problem. On the Sabbath morning, the family met in the parlor to leave the house together five minutes before the hour of public worship, to arrive at the meetinghouse two minutes before Mr. Stearns opened the ceremony. After the afternoon service, they rested briefly before meeting for evening prayers, when the children told their father what they had learned during the day. Samuel spent a few minutes explaining to them how to be saved and how to recognize salvation in the people they met. Sabbath ended with a hymn and a prayer at sundown.

Samuel Stearns explained to adults his concept of the Calvinist ministry when he preached in Milton at the ordination of Samuel

Gile, a pupil of Jonathan French. A minister, he said, must have had a religious experience which led to his justification, or assurance, in order to know how to teach it to others and to understand how effective it was in dealing with the problems of life. One without an experience was apt to misinterpret the Scriptures, be caught up in intellectual faddism, and teach untruths, to the loss both of himself and of the souls who heard him. Moreover, he was the presiding officer for all church business and worship services. In the temple, he must teach God had been offended by sinful man in a sinful world and explain the way to be received by God. It lay through penance, belief in God's power, Christ's mediation in one's behalf, a rebirth of knowledge and spirit, and an assurance that the rebirth was genuine. Listeners would not like what they heard, but a minister was not to sacrifice both their souls and his own by withholding the truth. In speaking to a group, the minister must adapt to the individual differences before him. He was to comfort the righteous and admonish the wicked, showing to them the need for conversion and demanding their compliance with the terms. During his pastoral visits, he was not to be austere, but show Christian dignity and watch for an opportunity to give the conversation an evangelical turn. For his work, a minister could expect God's support during his labors and a crown of glory as bright as an eternal star in the life after his labor had ended.

Two tenets in this formula for a religious life were to lead both to Samuel Stearns's success and to his failure. One was the insistence that both penance and faith were necessary for acceptance among God's people, and the second was that not insisting on this formula was a sin leading to destruction of one's audience and one's self.

It was shortly after the adoption of the new covenant that Mr. Stearns ceased reading the confessions of his congregation before the group in the meetinghouse. Instead, he carried cases of discipline to the church. This practice he based on procedure described in Matt.18:15–17. First one went to the offender privately, then in the company of two or three, and at last one brought the matter before the church. Early in his administration, he had several problems of discipline, and the case of William Merriam became tragic.

William was the youngest child of John and Abigail Merriam. Because those nearest him in age did not live, and the older children soon established homes of their own, William's boyhood was that of an only child. He listened to the discussion about baptism in 1765 and later, agreeing with his sister Lydia's husband, Nathaniel Sherman, that infants ought not to be subjected to the rite. In 1764 Rhode Island College, now Brown University, had been founded as a Baptist school, and as soon as William could, he enrolled there. However, his education was interrupted, probably by the death of his father, and he did not complete the course he had commenced. When he was twenty, he married Esther Bellamy, a woman he loved deeply.

William and Esther settled on the farm of his grandfather, the Deacon. Five children were born to them. Joseph Penniman was preaching in Bedford's pulpit, and the Merriams listened. Three weeks after the death of Joseph's daughter Molly, William's son, William Bellamy, died. The epitaph written for the little boy was a reasonable statement of the parents' attitude toward their loss, as Molly's had been the cry of mournful parents:

Hic est Sepultus; meum Glorium mundi
Here lies Buried
the Body of William
Bellamy Meriam
son of Mr. William
Meriam & Mrs
Esther his wife
who Died Sept: 7th
1778, Aged 25
months & one day.
Sleep on sweet Babe & take
your Rest,
God called you soon because
t'is best.

(Fig. 40)

The townsmen respected William, and he was named to various committees, to the office of selectman, and town clerk, a post he held for several years. He was a lieutenant in the Minute Men during the Revolutionary War.

The Merriams lost another son when he was only two years old. On his tombstone the parents again expressed their sense of loss:

Fig. 40. Tombstone of William Bellamy Merriam (1971 photograph)

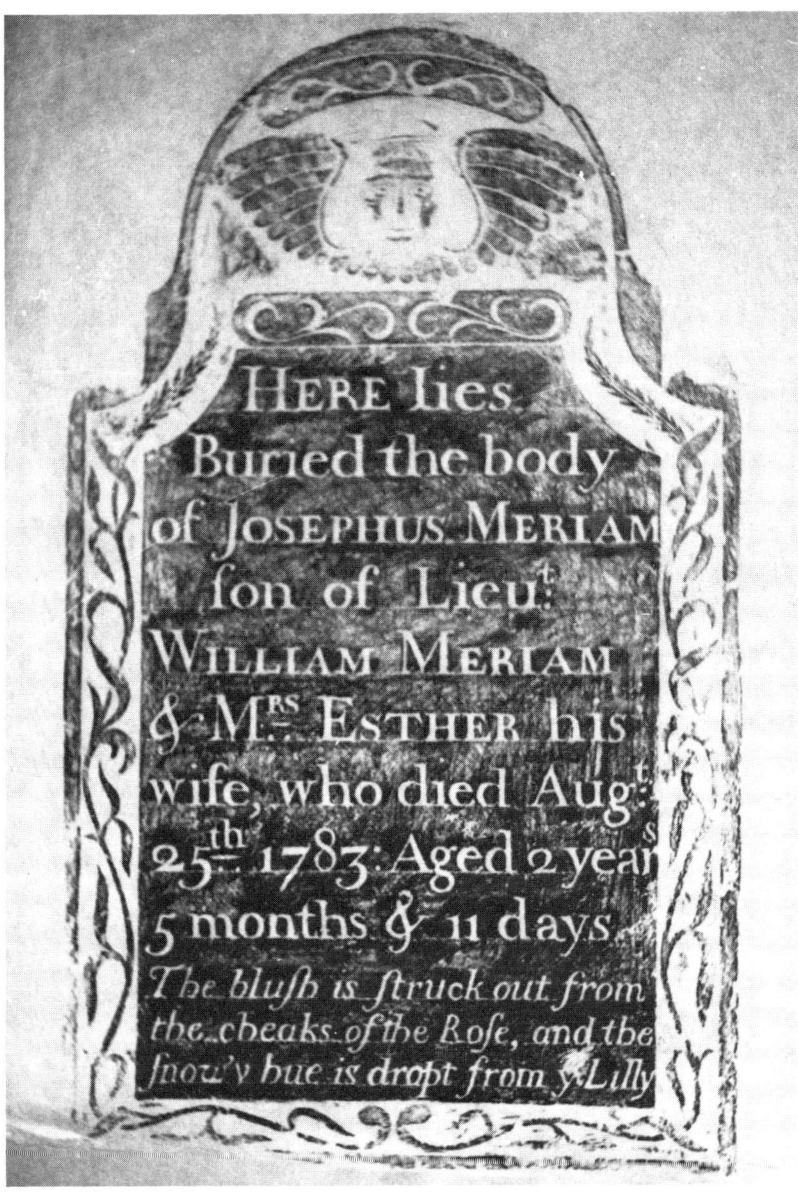

Fig. 41. Tombstone of Josephus Merriam (from a 1971 rubbing)

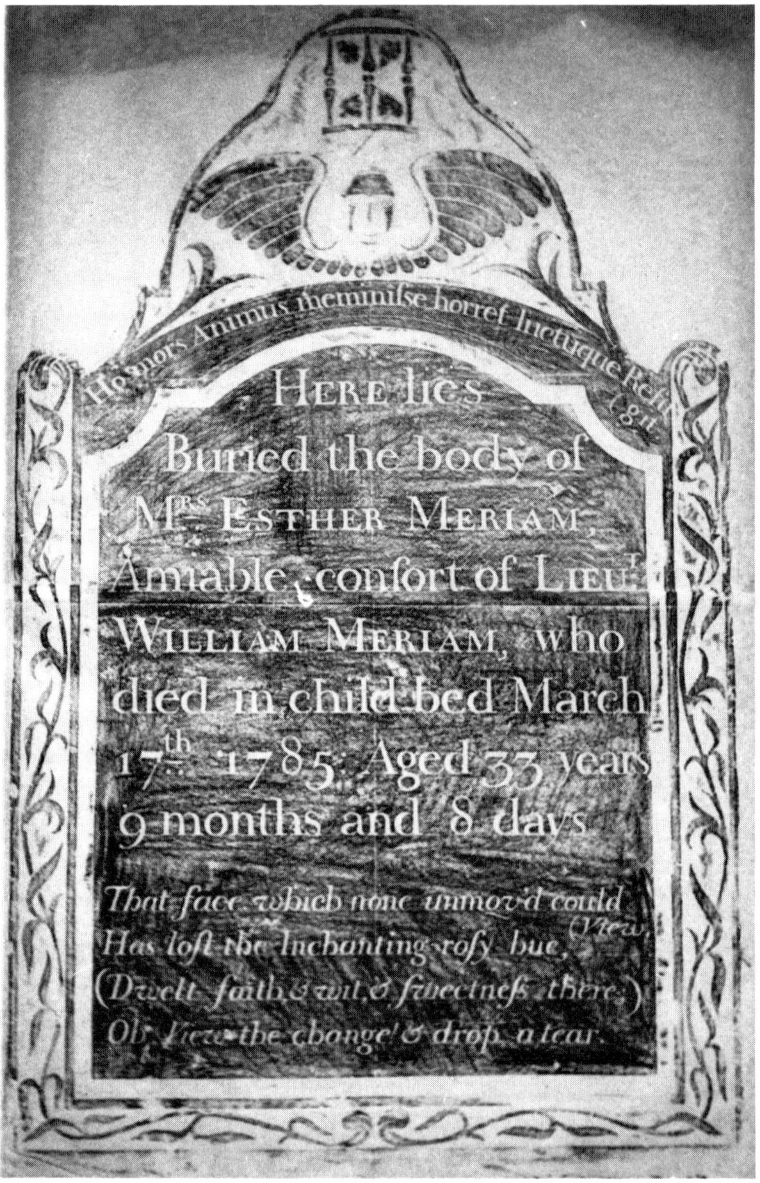

Fig. 42. Esther Merriam's tombstone (from a 1971 rubbing)

Here lies
Buried the body
of Josephus Meriam
son of Lieut:
William Meriam
& Mrs Esther his
wife, who died Augt:
25th 1783: aged 2 years
5 months & 11 days.
The blush is struck out from
The cheaks of the rose, and the
snow'y hue is dropt from ye Lilly.

(Fig. 41)

When their fifth child was born, Esther died, and William wept. He enumerated her admirable qualities on her stone, her complexion, her sweetness, her wit, and her faith:

Ho mors Animus meminisse horret luctuque refugit
Here lies
Buried the body of
Mrs Esther Meriam,
Amiable consort of Lieut:
William Meriam, who
died in child-bed March
17th 1785: Aged 33 years,
9 months and 8 days,
That face which none unmov'd could view,
Has lost the Inchanting rosy hue,
(Dwelt faith, & wit, & sweetness there;)
Oh View the change: & drop a tear.

After a respectful period, William remarried, choosing a widow, Rebecca (Howe) Fiske, of Lexington. She had two children, who probably came to Bedford to live with William's three, and Rebecca and William had three daughters, completing a family of eight.

Even through Mr. Penniman's trial and dismissal, William continued to work for the church, serving on the committee to treat with Mr. Stearns, and being named deacon.

The Merriams' youngest daughter died after the church had

rewritten its covenant, and her epitaph indicates William had been listening to the teaching of Samuel Stearns:

<pre>
              In memory of
           Louisa Howe Merriam
          daugr of Deacn William
           & Mrs Rebekah Merriam
          who died July 2, 1799
                aged 6 years
                 & 9 months
          To Jesus arms we recomend
        Thy nimble wit; thy active limb,
       Till that bright morn shall wake the
                        (slumbring clay
        To bloom & sparkle in eternal day.
</pre>

William came into another period of religious conflict when two of his oldest children married into the family of the Reverend Phineas Whitney, of Shirley, Massachusetts. His wife Lydia was the daughter of the Old Light, Nicholas Bowes, and Phineas was an Arminian. It was probably from them that William became convinced that faith was the only requirement for a saintly life. God helped all who had faith.

As the United States became a sovereign country and the Commonwealth of Massachusetts a distinct state, William became active in politics. He was a democrat, believing the strength of the nation was in the man who operated a small farm. He felt the national government should be limited in power, and the states, looking to their farms, should be as independent as possible in a union. He became the leader of the local democratic party.

He also began to question some of the teachings of Mr. Stearns, especially that stressing penance as a requirement for salvation. William rejected the thought that only those who grieved over their fallen state would be saved, and he defended faith as the key to God's grace.

Samuel realized that William had adopted Antinominianism, a state wherein one believed his actions were directed by the Holy Spirit. A believer in such a tenet had none of the humility of a penitent person. This belief had been observed among the ancient

Gnostics, the 16-century Anabaptists, and in the case of Anne Hutchinson. Now, somewhat modified, Mr. Stearns saw it in the current Arminianism and Universalism which were spreading around him. He could not have a deacon who accepted it, and when he could not convince William of his error, he took the case before the church. The members removed William from his office. He was also suspended from communion, and he was not reelected to town office.

Soon after, William's sister Anna lost her husband, Thomas Page, and began to put her estate in order. Anna was seventy-two, and she had lived through all the religious life of the town except its first seven years. She understood the only cost to the town for public worship service was the minister's salary, and she foresaw the day when the townsmen would refuse to pay for any sectarian minister. She prepared her will, leaving her property as a fund to support the ministry, planning thus to ensure the continuance of that office forever; and she gave a silver flagon to the church, as her grandfather had given a silver cup.

Anna marked her husband's grave in the simplest manner:

In Memory of
Mr. Thomas Page
who died
July 21, 1809
aged 76.

When William's stepdaughter died, her tombstone was erected beside the others of William's family.

In
memory of
Mrs Elizabeth Whitney,
wife of
Lieut. William Whitney,
who died
Feb. 24, 1810
aged 27.
Unvail thy bosom faithful tomb
Take their new treasure to thy trust
And give those sacred relicts room
To slumber in the silent dust.

At this time, William became irritable, a condition which worsened, until Rebecca was concerned and an arrangement was made that David Bacon would live in the Merriam household to "take the oversight" of William. To William, this was intolerable. He moved to his daughter Esther's home about a mile away.

William seemed calm when he retired on Sunday evening, June 24, 1810. "But rising in the morning before the family were up [Esther had seven children], and finding a gun, powder, and balls, having possessed himself of these, he set out across the fields for his own house; where it seems he secreted himself behind a wall, at a few rods distance from the house, and awaited an opportunity to effect his . . . design. In this position he continued, according to his own account, nearly an hour, when discovering [Mr. Bacon] as he was going from the house to the barn, he instantly shot him through the body." Mr. Merriam was intercepted "while in the act of charging again [perhaps] to dispatch next, either his wife or son . . ."

David Bacon died. Mr. Merriam was declared not sane and, because there was no established method of treatment or care, he was sent to West Port, New York, to live with his son Josephus and his wife Betsey (Rand).

On the Sabbath following David's death, Mr. Stearns preached from Exod.20:13, "Thou shalt not kill." His purpose was to define murder, to show various kinds of it, and to describe the sin of it. He offered sympathy first to David's friends and then to William's. To his church he said, "Dear brethren, I greatly fear lest we have failed in our duty towards him . . . we have not persevered in our supplications . . . that he might be . . . restored to the favor of God . . . In the day of solemn retribution some of us will be found wanting . . ."[7]

Mr. Stearns never wavered in believing both penance and faith were the requirements for a saintly life. However, he adopted milder rather than severer forms of evaluating them, probably soon after David's death.

Anna Merriam Page died two weeks after the tragedy. Someone arranged that her tombstone would say:

Erected
In memory of
Mrs. Anna Page
Relict of Mr. Thomas
Page, who died
July 10th, 1810.
Aet. 73
From Scenes of woe with sorrow prest,
She's bid adieu! and gone to rest.

Certainly Anna lately had known scenes of woe. After her property was settled, there was $663.93 for the ministerial fund. She required that it be "kept on interest . . . One-sixth part of the income arising therefrom shall be added to the principal as an increasing fund forever."* The remaining five-sixths of the interest was to be used to support the ministry. She believed the day would come when five-sixths of the interest would be larger than the ministerial salary. The surplus was to be expended for sacred music. However, over the years, the interest from the Page fund has been too meager to pay even a small portion of the ministerial salary.

Twice yearly in the meetinghouse Samuel held public examination of children in the catechism. First, he asked the formal questions in the document and then invited those who knew the entire contents to stand in the broad alley. Each child who repeated it perfectly was led to a "spectator's pew" because he would not be examined again. Of the smaller children, he asked simple questions based on principles of the Gospel. Everyone read the words of a hymn together. Samuel spoke to them about personal religion, using anecdotes and giving advice. He closed the service with prayer. His son William Augustus recited the entire catechism when he was six, and at fourteen he memorized the Gospel of Luke in a week.

Annually a committee bought the minister's wood from various townsmen and hauled it to Mr. Stearns's yard. Twenty cords made a row of logs 160 feet long, 4 feet high, and 4 feet wide. On a specified day, a group of residents came to cut the logs into sections appropriate for burning and to stack the firewood, probably in a

---

*The will of Anna Page is printed in the Appendix.

shed. The Stearns children remembered the day as one of activity, good cheer, and bantering. The number of children was increasing, and Josiah Atherton, Charlotte Esther, Ann Catherine, and Ebenezer S. completed the family of five sons and six daughters.

Moses Fitch, husband of Samuel's cousin, was named deacon in William Merriam's place, and the town's bass viol was put in the care of the elder deacon, James Wright. Samuel's cousin William had the care of the meetinghouse, opening and shutting the door and windows when necessary; sweeping the lower floor six times and the upper three times a year, before communion days; brushing the railings of the pews and cobwebs from the windowsills and canopy; and clearing the snow from the doors. For this he received about $3.75 a year.

In 1811, Solomon Lane, Samuel's brother-in-law, and Deacon Fitch asked the townsmen to review Mr. Stearns's salary. They voted to discontinue the foods, to set the salary at $560 a year with twenty cords of wood, and to continue the $1,000 loan.

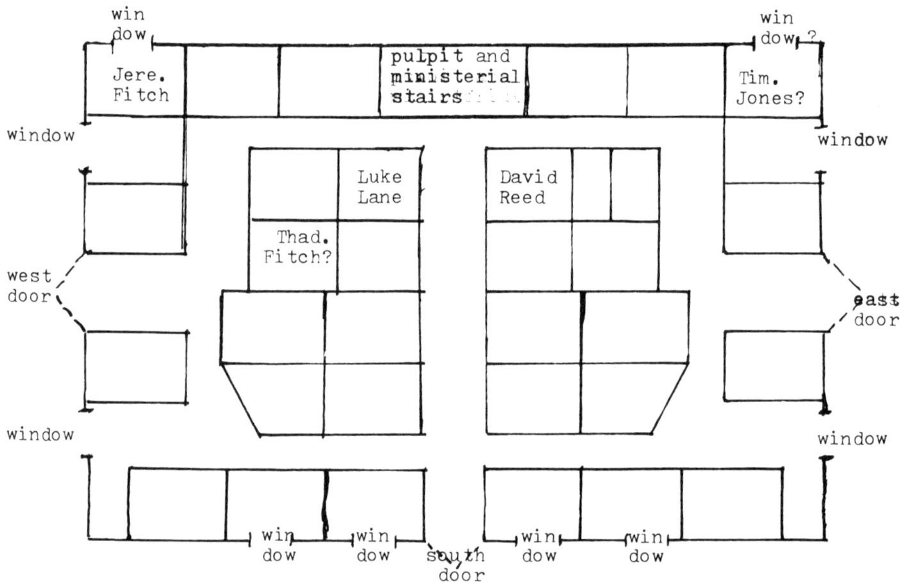

Fig. 43. Sale of pew ground, 1812, and other late changes*
(drawn from information in Bedford town records)
* Scale: 8 feet to 1 inch

The townsmen decided to sell more pew ground in 1813. (Fig. 43) They removed the two seats on either side of the middle alley in front of the pulpit, the last town's seats for the congregation (Fig. 44), and sold the ground under them for $48.75 to Captain David Reed and Luke Lane. There was no more pew ground on the floor. Space for pews in the east and west galleries was to be sold, but for some reason it was not, either then or at a later time. The townsmen tried to reseat the singers once more, but that plan was unclear and it failed.

While the meetinghouse was being rearranged, Mr. Stearns drove to Dunstable, New Hampshire, to preach the ordaining sermon for Ebenezer Sperry. Mrs. Sperry was his sister-in-law, Mary, and probably Samuel enjoyed that day.

But the next spring, when he went to Burlington for the ordination of Samuel Sewall, he became distressed. Mr. Sewall had been trained for the Episcopal ministry, but had found stumbling blocks in the Book of Common Prayer and had changed to Congregationalism. Samuel suspected Mr. Sewall had rejected not only the Book

Fig. 44. A seat said to have been used in the first meeting-house, having the date 1728 carved into the back.

of Common Prayer, but also the concept of the Trinity. For this reason, when Mr. Sewall had read his profession of faith before the council, Samuel Stearns asked permission to question him. The moderator at first hesitated and then admitted the question so that the council could rule on its appropriateness. Samuel asked whether the candidate "believed that the future punishment of the wicked would be of equal duration with the happiness of the righteous." The moderator cried, "O Brother Stearns: I knew your question would be an improper one, and I won't put it." [8]

Samuel rose and left the meeting. Two other ministers followed him. They believed any answer to the question would have shown whether Mr. Sewall understood the tenet of salvation through penance and faith, and they would not ordain anyone whose philosophy was not known.

Mr. Sewall was not hurt, but amused.* The council itself had been carefully balanced with seven "avowed Unitarians," seven "Orthodox," and a moderator. Jedidiah Morse, the Orthodox Congregationalist of Charlestown, was a member, but he did not walk away.

Later Samuel wrote to Mr. Morse, wishing to be reassured that he had not been too severe. Jedidiah replied that Samuel had been honest, but the right of the council to question may have been denied. He suggested Samuel take that matter up with his ministerial association. Meanwhile, when Samuel could come to Charlestown for a night, he would explain why he himself had not walked away.

On April 1, 1815, Elijah Stearns, cousin and neighbor of Samuel, and thirteen others sponsored Article 6 in the warrant for a town meeting, "To know if it be the mind of the town to build a new meetinghouse and make arrangements for the purpose or do anything respecting a meetinghouse." The town appointed a committee "to take into consideration the expediency of the building and what the old house will fetch and report to the town at next May meeting." [9]

The committee's report, submitted on May 1, was unacceptable, probably because it contained no details. However, during the fol-

---

* Later Mr. Sewall and Samuel Stearns were to become friends.

lowing season, detailed plans were worked out, including a sketch of the proposed building.

In September an event occurred which may have influenced the size of the building being considered, the kind of wood to be used, and the speed with which the work could be done. It was the great gale of 1815.

◂§ The summer . . . was remarkable for . . . violent and disastrous storms . . . The equinoctial gale of September, however, exceeded them all in violence, and caused greater . . . disaster than any . . . since the settlement of the country.

The storm began at three o'clock on the morning of Friday, the twenty-second when the wind was at the northeast, and rain fell copiously until sunrise. During the forenoon . . . rain fell to a considerable amount. In the afternoon the wind blew with increased force, and rain continued to fall . . . Before sunrise . . . the wind again became violent having changed to the east in the night . . . about nine o'clock was very strong . . . At ten o'clock it shifted to the southeast, and continued to increase in force until it blew so fiercely that buildings, fences, trees, vessels . . . were swept away . . . The wind . . . came in gusts, and continued its work of destruction until noon, when it changed to the southwest . . . Before night pleasant weather had come.

During the heaviest part of the gale fires could not exist in the houses, being blown out as fast as they were lighted . . . The air . . . was very oppressive and almost suffocating . . . This wind . . . prostrated the great oaks and pines . . .

As blast after blast of wind blew down buildings, the people closed windows and doors .   If the windows and doors on the leeward side of the buildings had been left open a far less number of roofs would have been blown off . . .

The countenances of the people . . . bore an expression of awe and fear. Each one thought that his house might be the next one to be shattered to atoms . . .

The gale was felt as far south as Delaware.[10] ◊►

In Bedford, an old garrison house on the west end of the road to Concord was destroyed. It had been Jonathan Woolley's place, and probably had been built about 1680 by the original covenantor,

Joseph French, a housewright. The meetinghouse may have been damaged. The woodland was injured, but it was turned into a source of lumber for many building projects.

The town committee's plan for the meetinghouse was "that the house be built 58 feet long and 53 feet wide, 30-foot posts, projection 34 feet by 8 feet. Close stairs to the pulpit; 58 pews on the lower floor; to be glazed with glass 10 inches by 13 inches, 24 lights in a window . . . underpinned with 2 tiers of good and well-hewn stone, each tier . . . 14 inches deep, with 3 door steps, the whole to conform to a plan now . . . presented for inspection . . . the undertakers to have the old meetinghouse and being allowed to use whatever is suitable for said work." The price they were considering was $2,500. The meetinghouse was to "front the road leading from Carlisle to Lexington and . . . to be set 40 feet south from the front of the old meetinghouse."

The detailed plan was accepted and the same committee was asked "to let out the building of said house."[11]

Many years later, when students of architecture examined the meetinghouse, they recognized that many features of the building were similar to illustrations in a book of plans for churches which was written by Asher Benjamin to assist carpenters, especially country artisans, in their work.[12] The porch and tower are like those on the West Street Church in Boston, and it is now assumed that Mr. Benjamin's book was used as a guide in building both that church and the second meetinghouse in Bedford.

The contract for construction was given to Joshua Page, great-grandson of the first covenantor, Nathaniel, and Levi Wilson, grandson of Jonathan Wilson, who had been killed on April 19, 1775. The cost had risen to $5,445 plus the old building, which would supply timbers useful in the construction of the new.

In the spring, townsmen appointed building inspectors, and changing the site, decided to set the meetinghouse south of the elm trees which stood south of the old meetinghouse, so that the body of the house ranged with the trees, fronting north.

The frame of the eighty-seven-year old building was stripped to its timbers early in July 1816, after the last public worship service was held in it. Later Samuel's son William Augustus remembered how the interior of the old house had felt to a small boy:

~§ In the interior of the house the pulpit stood on the north side, next the road. In the front was a gallery of pews; on the left hand, a gallery of long seats which the singers occupied; on the right, a gallery, mostly filled by single men, who had no other seat . . . Up over the front gallery, in the ceiling, was a scuttle, opening, if it were ever opened, into the roof. It had a mysterious look to children, and I used to hear it said sometimes in the village that it was the place where the tithingman put naughty boys. I believe the town powder was kept up there for some years. The pews below were square, high, and with bannisters under the railing, which the children, when standing, could look through, and would amuse themselves with turning and squeaking when they could do it with impunity. The seats of the pews, rarely cushioned, were hung on hinges, so that they could be turned up for comfort in standing during the long prayer, "which often reached half an hour in length." Oh, I remember, as though it were yesterday, how those seats used to come clattering down when the prayer was over, as if they were saying, according to the different spirit of the worshippers, "Amen, amen; glad you are done, glad you are done; amen!" The house never had a fire in it, and in the winter, oh so cold! I see the minister, with the thermometer down to zero, with coat, cloak, and gloves on, and handkerchief round his neck, till thawed out by the warmth of his subject, he threw some of them off. I hear the men, in such weather, knocking their feet together, here and there over the house, during the latter half of the sermon, as if they were saying, "Oh, do stop; I shall freeze to death if you do not say, Amen soon!" I hear the windows rattle, and the howl of the storm without, and almost shiver just as I used to, as I sat, curled up in solemn endurance, looking sometimes wishfully at the footstove, which it was my privilege to carry, but, being a boy, not often to enjoy.[13] ̧~

Townsmen gathered on July eighth to pull sections of the new building into place and returned nine days later for a thanksgiving held on its floor. The work progressed so well that the completion date was moved from November 1, 1817, to July 1. The cost was increased when they changed the doorsteps from two feet wide to two and a half feet. The old, cracked bell had been sold from storage, and the money it brought was in a bell fund. The townsmen voted to add $350 to the fund and asked three men to procure a new bell for the tower on the new house.

When work on the interior began, the townsmen voted to have a circular stairway to the pulpit and to remove the free seats near it to the foot of the broad aisle. This added $92 to the cost of the building.

In the spring a committee was to see that the common was leveled and the ground around the meetinghouse was built up. This they were unable to do with volunteer labor and the cost was charged to the polls and estates of the inhabitants.

Details absorbed the attention of the townsmen. They voted that thanks be presented to Mr. Jeremiah Fitch, of Boston, for his friendly assistance in negotiating for a bell at England and other favors, and that Samuel Stearns deliver them accordingly. Five men were to bring the bell from Boston and to hang it on the meetinghouse in a manner they thought would be beneficial to the town.

They decided the cost of mahogany railings for the desk and pews would come from money raised by selling pews. They would allow ten dollars for music for the dedication of the building. James Wright, Jr., the Deacon's son, was charged with performing the duties of custodian for $11.25 a year, a considerably higher figure than Samuel Stearns's cousin William had earned in the old meetinghouse. The duties were the same, except that James had the added responsibility of ringing the new bell twice in the forenoon and twice in the afternoon and on occasion at funerals.

At this time also, Michael Crosby was named by the church to replace Deacon Wright, who was not well.

They wrote rules for the use of the building, "no town meetings, no training, nor choosing militia officers shall ever be held or done in the meetinghouse, and no other town business shall be done in said house except by permission of the selectmen for the time being . . . no person shall hang his hat or hats on any post or on the wall of the house or on any other machine above the railings of the pews on the lower floor in the body of said meetinghouse or on the front of the galleries or on the walls of the galleries." [14]

The new meetinghouse was to be a building for the use of the church only.

Fifty-six long, straight pews and the alleys to serve them filled the floor of the house and sixteen pews were completed in the galleries, although several more could have been built there. They were slip pews separated one from another by a closed end, and each seated six or more people. Their legs, about 2 inches by 4 inches in cross section, were countersunk through holes of similar size and shape in the floor.* Probably gates were hung across the ends of the pews which opened into the alleys.

A committee of eleven was formed to appraise the pews and to arrange that they be sold on July 1, 1817. The total value of the pews was to be equal to the cost of the new meetinghouse, or $6,101. The price of each pew varied from $25 to $134, depending on its location on the floor of the house. Pew number 20 was set aside as a ministerial pew to be owned by the town and valued at $99. The seventy-two pews were appraised at $6,222, from which $99 was deducted, since pew number 20 was not sold, leaving $6,123 or $22 above the committee's goal.

Moreover, they used the occasion of the sale as an opportunity to raise money for a fund for the church. Prospective pew owners bid at vendue not on the price of the pews, which had been pre-determined by the committee, but for a choice of the pews for sale. One man paid $40 for the choice of pew Number 19, which was worth $99. The money collected from bids on choice was $1,000, and the town kept it in a separate list for the use of the church. David Reed, Jr., gave an account of the two funds, proceeds of the sale, to the town clerk, William Webber, who entered them in his book along with the names of the pew owners.

Fifty-six men bought the seventy-one pews; no women bid on any. Some of the buyers wanted to use their pews, some bought them for the ladies in their families, and some were contributing money for the new meetinghouse in their town. The buyers were:

> Bacon, Benjamin, Jr., grandson of Deacon Benjamin
> Bacon, Elijah, son of Benjamin, Jr.
> Bacon, Thompson, uncle of Benjamin, Jr.
> Blodgett, Simeon, husband of Sally Fitch, probably grand-
> daughter of Joseph Fitch

---

* The holes in the floor are still there.

Brown, Joseph, husband first of Betsey Wright, daughter of
      Deacon James, and second of Rachel Fitch, daughter of
      Deacon Moses
Buttrick, Willard, father of a family who had moved from
      Concord by 1801
Crosby, Deacon Michael, taking the place of Deacon James
      Wright
Davis, Eleazer, great-grandson of the first covenantor, Eleazer
Fitch, Alford, nephew of Deacon Moses Fitch
Fitch, David, great-grandson of the first covenantor, Samuel
      Fitch
Fitch, Jeremiah, brother of Alford
Fitch, Joel, son of Deacon Moses Fitch
Fitch, Deacon Moses, grandson of the first convenantor, Samuel
      Fitch
Fitch, Moses, Jr., son of Deacon Moses Fitch
Gooding, William, perhaps Goodrich, pew owner in the first
      meetinghouse
Hartwell, William, Jr, greatgrandson of the first covenantor,
      William
Hayward, Mather, husband of Lucy Page
Hill, Josiah, descendant of the neighbor of Obed Abbott
Jones, John, probably related to Lieutenant Timothy Jones
Jones, Timothy, son of Lieutenant Timothy Jones
Lane, David, son of James and Mary (Wellington) Lane
Lane, Eliab B., great-grandson of the first covenantor, John
      Lane
Lane, Job, greatgrandson of Deacon Job Lane
Lane, Jonathan, great-grandson of Deacon Job Lane
Lane, Roger, brother of Eliab
Lane, Solomon, brother of David
Lane, Stephen, grandson of Deacon Job Lane
Mead, Asa, great-grandson of the first covenantor, Daniel
      Cheever
Merriam, John, great-grandson of Deacon Nathaniel Merriam
Page, Joshua, great-grandson of the first covenantor, Nathaniel
      Page
Page, Moses, brother of Joshua

Page, Nathaniel, Jr., great-grandson of the first covenantor,
    Nathaniel Page
Pollard, Obed, descendant of Walter or Oliver Pollard
Pollard, Oliver, descendant of Walter or Oliver Pollard
Preston, Doctor Amariah, husband of Ruhamah Lane, sister of
    Eliab Lane
Price, David, named on tax lists
Putnam, Jonas, husband of Hannah Evans, niece of Samuel
    Hartwell
Reed, David, distant relative of John Reed, Esq.
Reed, David, Jr., son of David
Reed, John, son of John, Esq., or of David
Robinson, Jesse, named on tax lists
Sage, Samuel, recently come from England
Simonds Benjamin, father of a family who had moved from
    Woburn in 1805
Simonds, Benjamin, Jr., son of Benjamin
Simonds, Zebedee, son of Benjamin, to be named deacon
Skelton, Daze, husband of Ruth Hartwell
Skelton, Elijah, probably son of Daze
Spaulding, Sampson, a Billerica man who came to Bedford to
    worship
Sprague, Loel, named on tax lists
Stearns, Elijah, cousin of Samuel Stearns
Stearns, Simeon, brother of Elijah
Webber, James, son of John and Sarah (Fassett) Webber
Webber, John, brother of James
Webber, William, brother of James
Wilson, Levi, contractor of the meetinghouse
Wright, James, Jr., son of Deacon James Wright[15]

The Bacons bought three pews; Deacon Crosby bought four; the
Fitch family, seven; Mr. Hayward, two; the Lanes, seven; Mr. Merriam, two; the Pages, four; the Reeds, seven; the Simonds family,
four; the Skeltons, three; the Stearns family, two, while the minister
had the use of one; and the Webbers, three.

The dedication of the building was held on July 8, 1817, one
week after the sale of pews. Mr. Stearns preached from Gen.28:17:

Fig. 45. The second meetinghouse in Bedford, 1817-18
(1973 photograph)

"This is none other but the house of God, and this is the gate of heaven." He said houses of worship were like temples and tabernacles, places where God held communion with the Elect, where purity of worship was maintained, where ordinances were administered, where God dwelt. If His word and ordinances were not administered in purity, His gracious presence would be withdrawn. Then the house would be a monument to folly and sin. Each person should bring into the new temple a new and sanctified heart, and pray that He bless the ordinances in His house so that it might be the gate of heaven. (Fig. 45)

Now Mr. Stearns organized a Sunday School, one of the first in Massachusetts, with books, classes, teachers, and a superintendent. With a bit of ceremony, on Sabbaths the children met with their teachers in the center schoolhouse, which stood several rods northeast of the meetinghouse, while the Stearns family gathered in their parlor northwest of the church. At a designated time the Stearns procession walked up the road to the land around the meetinghouse. James Wright, Jr., rang the bell; the Sunday School classes, led by the teachers, fell in line behind the minister, and the company marched into the church.

In 1821, when Samuel had preached for twenty-five years, the covenant of the church was published with a list of membership. There were one hundred and five members, thirty-nine men and sixty-six women. Twenty-six were descendants of the founding covenantors and twenty-six owned pews. Sixty-seven members were in twelve large families. A few were unattached persons, new to the town, while other new names were those who had married into Bedford families.

There were one hundred and fifty-five polls in Bedford that year,* proprietors, widows owning property, heirs, and guardians, who paid the town's expenses, including the ministerial salary. Twenty-nine taxpayers were members of the church, while thirteen male members were not taxed, either because they lived elsewhere or because they owned nothing taxable.

When Deacon Moses Fitch died at seventy-one, Zebedee Simonds was named to take his place, but Mr. Simonds lived only eight months after his election, and Amos Hartwell, twenty-seven, was

---

* The polls are in the town clerk's office, Bedford.

chosen to work with Deacon Michael Crosby. Amos was the great-grandson of the first covenantor, William Hartwell.

Perhaps some members of the singing school were not attending public worship services. In any case, townsmen worked out an agreement with the school, called the "Harmonic Society," whereby some income from the Page fund and twenty-five dollars raised by the school was used for music. The school declared its purpose to be the encouragement of sacred music, which they looked upon as an essential part of public worship, and its members were to sit in the seats allotted to singers and be absent only if it was unavoidable. There were twenty-two men and fifteen women in the school, but only three were members of the church.

The uses of the new bell were separated into two functions. The custodian of the meetinghouse rang it on Sabbaths and Lecture Days; another person rang it at noon, at nine o'clock in the evening, and at funerals when requested.

The problems with the attendance of the singers on Sabbaths and the separation of the use of the bell into religious and secular functions may have been symptoms of an uneasy unhappiness caused by the lack of religious freedom in the town. On April 3, 1824, Benjamin Bacon III, great-grandson of Deacon Benjamin and Catherine (Lane) Bacon, a young man of twenty-three whose father and brother were members of Samuel Stearns's church, brought a certificate to the town clerk which read: "This is to certify that Benjamin Bacon 3rd of the town of Bedford is a member of the religious society called the First Universalist Society in Cambridge—by order of the standing Committee—Josiah Macon, Jr." It was the first of several certificates the town clerk recorded in his book. William Page became a member of the Congregational Society in Lexington; Lewis Bemis joined the Methodist-Episcopal Church in Weston; George Sloane and Edward Flint became members of the Universalist Society in Stoneham.[16] The polls in the town were dividing.

Samuel Stearns probably was aware of the growing dissatisfaction. He wanted to counteract it, and thought he had found a way when he heard of Mr. Lyman Beecher's progress in fighting Unitarianism in Boston.

The Reverend Lyman Beecher, father of Henry Ward Beecher, Harriet Beecher Stowe, and other children who became well known, had moved from a pulpit in Litchfield, Connecticut, to the Hanover

Street Church in Boston in 1826 to establish an alternative to the Unitarian movement in that city. Mr. Beecher was a Calvinist and a revival preacher. "Having declared war on infidelity, dueling, and drinking while he was in Connecticut, Lyman Beecher next attacked Unitarianism at the citadel of its power in Boston," [17] his grandson was to say. Mr. Beecher conducted the services in his churches at a constant level of revivalism. He believed everyone had enough freedom of will to follow God's laws for regeneration, justification, and salvation. He attributed this belief, a tenet of the form of Calvinism called Edwardianism, to Jonathan Edwards's teachings of seventy-five years before. It was an easement in the helpless bound of predestination, even as Peter Bulkeley had described one when he had said a reasonable God wanted to be in covenant with all his people.

Mr. Beecher worked both in and around Boston. "I preach every Thursday evening at Cambridgeport, a mile only this side of the college, in the Baptist meetinghouse . . . A revival is begun—about a dozen inquirers, and five cases of recent and joyful hope . . ." One who listened to him in the Hanover Street Church was Dr. James P. Chaplin, of Cambridgeport. "He had been in the habit of listening to a dead, feeble fellow on the wrong side, but who didn't do much for any side . . . He began to bring over his family and his patients from Cambridgeport; and, as the seriousness increased, he came in with three or four carriages—some thirty persons—every Sabbath." [18]

Lyman Beecher "set-off" twenty-five persons to "colonize" Cambridgeport, probably in 1829. In the spring of 1831, he held a protracted meeting, a revival meeting of several consecutive days' duration, in Boston, inviting famous revivalists from New York and Connecticut to come to preach. Dr. Nathaniel William Taylor, President of Yale Theological Seminary, and the Reverend Charles Finney, a popular revivalist preacher from the State of New York, were among them. Mr. Finney spoke in Park Street Church and other churches while he was in Boston.

It is not surprising that some of the members of the Bedford Church heard of Mr. Beecher's protracted meeting and wanted to have one in their town. Whether the plan was first proposed by Samuel Stearns is not known, but he gave it his complete support.

The church held a meeting to discuss the plan. Those in favor said it would quicken their spirit and benefit their neighbors. Those opposed pointed out that it would further divide the town, or parish, as they were calling the entire religious community, bringing criticism on Mr. Stearns and causing his contract to be questioned. Events were to show they appraised the effect of the plan correctly.

Mr. Stearns felt the church should consider only the benefits of a revival in Bedford. The church supported him, voting for it to be held early in October 1831. The meeting may have continued for eight days, from Sabbath to Sabbath.

In the first week of November, Samuel received a notice that a public lecture would be held in the Town Hall on Wednesday, November 16, when the Reverend Mr. Smith of the First Universalist Church of Woburn would speak on Universal Salvation.

On Monday, the fourteenth, the townsmen were asked to vote on the request of Thompson Bacon and twenty-three others, "To know if the town will grant the use of the meetinghouse in said town for the use of a preacher of the Unitarian denomination on the first two Sabbaths of December, January, March, and April." [19] The townsmen voted, sixty-five to forty-two, that the request be granted.

This action contained a double thrust. First, it called for Unitarian preaching, scholarly and logical, in contrast to the revival meeting, evangelical and emotional, which had recently been held in the meetinghouse; and secondly, the Unitarian preaching was to happen eight times, perhaps in exact balance for the protracted meeting.

But there was the matter of the pulpit, a pulpit denied to Whitefield by Nicholas Bowes, opened to neighboring preachers during the ministry of Joseph Penniman, and now under contract to Samuel Stearns. The townsmen asked Thompson Bacon, his son Reuben, who was the town clerk, and Deacon Amos Hartwell, as a committee, to see that the Unitarian ministers were brought into the meetinghouse "in such a manner as shall be deemed most conciliatory and proper." [20] They wanted no public disturbance about the use of the pulpit.

Reuben, as town clerk, sent a copy of the town's vote to Samuel, and the committee called upon him to arrange for the town's use of the pulpit. They invited his suggestions, asking him to voluntarily give up the pulpit on the specified days, and said he could preach in the Town Hall on those occasions.

Mr. Stearns reported the conversation to his church. He pointed out that eight Sabbaths were nearly one half the Sabbaths he ordinarily would preach in four months, and said the plan was interruptive and embarrassing to him. He had heard the rumor that the townsmen were dissatisfied because he did not exchange pulpits with others. He explained to his church that he had never exchanged indiscriminately. There were two Orthodox ministers about whom he was troubled and he would not exchange with them until his objections were removed. He did not name them, but it was later disclosed that they preached in Concord and Billerica. He concluded by saying that there were no leading doctrines on which he and the Unitarians agreed; however, he told them, he had acceded to the committee's request.

In his letter to the committee, he had written, "I stand ready to perform all ministerial duties to my people, on the Sabbath and at other times, in the pulpit, and in other places. I propose, without being understood thereby to surrender any of my just rights as the minister of this place, but to prevent contention on the Sabbath, peacefully to withdraw to the Town Hall, where I shall be happy to meet any such of my beloved flock as may assemble there." [21]

The committee replied to Samuel at length, but Deacon Hartwell, loyal to Mr. Stearns and the Edwardianism he taught, did not sign the letter. It was true, they wrote, that townsmen as a corporation had not criticized his custom of not exchanging pulpits. But he must know that "a large portion of your parishioners have for years been dissatisfied with the exclusive system pursued, and that many of the most respectable members of your church have frankly and unreservedly acknowledged to us that they should have no objections to your exchanging with ministers of the Unitarian denomination . . . One of the committee communicated the substance of the above to you . . . some months past . . . The committee had prepared [but did not send] a letter . . . to you . . . expressing a desire that something might be done to unite this little town in the bonds of Christian charity . . ." The committeemen further admitted now that they had made no arrangements to supply the pulpit on the days named by the town. And they suggested that if Mr. Stearns were willing to suspend his public worship services on those days and himself make arrangements for exchanges with Unitarian ministers, this action would tend "to cement the bonds of union and harmony; and that, for years to come, we might remain one undivided society, cheerfully contributing and administering to your comfort and happiness." [22]

Mr. Stearns took no steps to exchange with Unitarian ministers, however, and the committee informed him that the Reverend Ezra Ripley, of Concord, would preach in the meetinghouse on December 4, 1831.

The second Sabbath in December was communion day, and the committee, noting this, canceled plans for a visiting preacher. Mr. Stearns returned to his pulpit, and spirits were high. Some of the congregation decided to take a stand, and eighteen were admitted to membership of the church during the service. [23]

Other ministers visiting the pulpit during the winter were Nathaniel Whitman, of Billerica; Mr. Field, of "Westown"; S. Ripley, of Waltham, and C. Francis, of Watertown.

Just before the end of 1831, Samuel's second son, William Augustus, twenty-six, was ordained in the First Evangelical Church in Cambridgeport, Massachusetts, that had grown out of Lyman Beecher's "colonizing" efforts. A few years later, William was to write to Lyman: "Inclosed is a bank-note of one hundred dollars, which you will please accept, for your own use, from your friends in Cambridgeport. It is a feeble expression of obligations which we can never cancel. Not more than seven or eight years ago you went to war in this place at your charges. You fought a hard battle, and, through the blessing of God, gained a great victory. We enjoy, in consequence, peace and plenty." [24]

Early in 1832, Samuel Stearns heard a rumor that R.L.* and nine others were preparing an article for the town meeting on March 5, 1832, which would preclude the use of the Town Hall for religious meetings. He wrote to his son Samuel Horatio, who, it is believed, was preaching in Newburyport, asking him to come to the meeting. "There should be somebody there who can see and feel, and who can speak." (Mr. Stearns by custom could not address a town meeting, but Samuel Horatio was a resident of Bedford.) "An address . . . laying the subject open to the people, in all its bearings and consequences, may be of incalculable benefit . . ." At the end of February he announced to his church that the next two Sabbath

---

* This may have been Roger Lane.

services would be held in the Town Hall, though he did not know if they could be. It depended on the vote on March 5. He wished he could speak on the article. He wrote again to Samuel Horatio, asking him to come. "I renewed my cold," he added, "had a restless, or rather, sick night; today, am a little better. I often tremble lest I should be laid aside at this critical juncture . . ." [25] He was sixty-two and had preached thirty-five years.

He wrote to his son William Augustus at this time also. His church was now more than a hundred and sixty people, he wrote, all gathered during his ministry, except two aged females. At another time, speaking of his congregation, he said "four hundred and seventy of them had been consigned to the grave." [26]

There was a large gathering at the town meeting on March 5, and great excitement. Samuel Horatio spoke to the people at length. But the majority were impatient, and knew their strength. The wording of the article was changed, and it passed with a heavy vote.

Reuben Bacon sent a report to Mr. Stearns, saying there were seventy-one in favor of and forty-seven opposed to the rule that "no minority of the religious society in this town shall occupy the Town Hall on Lord's days, until it shall form a society, and file a certificate thereof in the clerk's office; and, when that shall have been done, said society shall have liberty to occupy said Hall during the pleasure of the town." [27] Reuben pointed out that the townsmen had taken the use of the Hall away from the committee, so the members would no longer be dealing with Mr. Stearns.

Nevertheless, this action pointed out a way for Mr. Stearns and his church to continue to meet, at least for a while. It was that the covenanted group become a society and file a certificate in the clerk's office. Henceforth, there would be two religious societies in Bedford, the Trinitarian Congregational Society and the First Parish, Unitarian.

Jeremiah Fitch, of Boston, who had helped procure a bell for the meetinghouse, heard of this. He had been born in the house next to that of the Stearns family, and Samuel had baptized him. Although his business was in Boston, he owned his boyhood home and stayed in Bedford whenever he could. He was a member of a Unitarian society in Boston and a lifelong member of the American Unitarian Association. Nevertheless, he said to a friend: "Do you suppose that I was going to suffer that good old man who put his hand on my forehead and baptized me in the name of the Father, Son, and Holy Ghost, to be turned out of town, and I not help him?" [28]

Jeremiah owned land across the road from the Stearns's home. He had said he never would sell it, but he gave some of it for the use of a second meetinghouse in Bedford, and a building may have been commenced there in 1832.

While it was being built, Mr. Stearns met his church in the meetinghouse one half of the time and in his home the other half. The doors of two rooms on either side of the front hall were opened for the use of the church and congregation, and the hall itself was filled. The singers sat in the upper hall, children on the stairs. The old minister arranged a small, high desk between the doors and the foot of the stairs. There, his gray hair parted on his broad forehead, his body thin and careworn, he conducted the services.

Samuel's salary was still paid from the town's tax funds, and because no one would pay more taxes to increase the fund for two ministerial salaries, there was pressure to abolish or diminish that of Mr. Stearns so that a Unitarian minister could be hired.

The townsmen asked Mr. Stearns to apply for a dismissal or to accept a reduction in salary, on the grounds that a large number of the parish had withdrawn and left his support principally upon the group who did not believe in all his doctrines.

Mr. Stearns retorted, "Church-members or others [who] have withdrawn from the parish . . . have acted in this case on their own responsibility . . . My salary . . . has never afforded me an adequate support without aid from other sources of supply . . . I wish . . . to be distinctly informed whether the parish have any articles of impeachment . . . against my moral or ministerial character . . ." [29] He said he would consent to a dismissal if both the parish and he could agree on the terms on which it should be done.

The townsmen asked him to accept part salary, saying they would give him a colleague. Then they voted to pay him through October 1832, provided he asked to be dismissed then. They reviewed the loan of $1,000 which had been granted him in 1801.

Mr. Stearns insisted he had performed no ecclesiastical sin; he was the same person, with philosophy and principles unchanged, that the town had hired thirty-six years before. He wanted the case brought before a council, since he felt he would be cleared of any possible charges. He said he would resign if either he were granted an annuity of half-salary, or the loan of $1,000 were canceled.

No settlement was reached, and any plans for a council meeting were delayed. During this time, still without a meetinghouse of their own, the men of Mr. Stearns's church met on November 8, 1832, at Fuller's Tavern and formed the Trinitarian Congregational Society.

At last a council meeting was arranged for Wednesday, February 27, 1833, at Mr. Fuller's house, probably also called Fuller's Tavern. Three Orthodox ministers and delegates from their churches were invited, John Codman and Isaac Howe, of the Second Church in Dorchester; Samuel Gile and Lewis Tucker, of Milton; and Warren Fay and John Doane, of the First Church in Charlestown. The three Unitarian ministers and delegates were James Walker and Charles Foster, of the Second Congregational Church in Charlestown; Ezra Stiles and James Savage, of the Federal Street Church of Boston; and Caleb Stetson and Abner Bartlett, of the First Church in Medford.

The moderator, a man pleasing to both Mr. Stearns and the group now called the First Parish, Unitarian, was Hosea Hildreth, of Gloucester.[30] Mr. Hildreth was perhaps the last of the school of Mr. Penniman's day, a man who did not approve of controversy or divisiveness. When he had been ordained in 1825 his council was composed of both ecclesiastical parties. He exchanged pulpits with both Orthodox and Unitarians, and people from both parties belonged to his church. Later he was disowned by the Essex Association for exchanging with Unitarians.

The question put before the council was, "Is it expedient, proper, and just that the relation of the Reverend Samuel Stearns to the First Congregational Society [the First Parish, Unitarian] in Bedford as pastor, be dissolved?"[31]

Mr. Stearns was represented by the Honorable Samuel Hoar and the Unitarians by the Honorable John Keyes, both of Concord.

The meeting opened with prayer by Mr. Hildreth. Then it adjourned to the Town Hall, probably because Fuller's house or tavern could not accommodate the crowd of spectators. After the morning session, there was a recess until 2:30 P.M. Following the afternoon session, the members rested for tea and met again at 7:15 P.M. During the evening Ezra Ripley, of Concord Church, and Nathaniel Whitman, of Billerica, testified, saying they were not at first considered Unitarians, but after they had preached for some time, their philosophies had changed. Then Samuel Stearns refused to exchange pulpits with them. The meeting went on until two o'clock in the morning.

The council reconvened at 8:30 A.M. on Thursday. The meeting opened with prayer by Dr. Codman, and the members wrote their report, affirming the expediency of severing the relationship between the First Congregational Society, now the First Parish, Unitarian, and Samuel Stearns. No charge had been sustained against the minister's moral character, nor was there any intent of a criminal charge against him:

> It is expedient and just that the relation of the Reverend Samuel Stearns of the First Congregational Society in Bedford as their pastor be dissolved on suitable pecuniary considerations, which will be:
> That the note for one thousand dollars held by the town or parish against the Reverend Samuel Stearns be cancelled and that:
> Mr. Stearns' salary from the time the Trinitarian Society was formed until the day when the connection is dissolved be assessed in two parts; the First Parish paying that part of the whole salary which is in proportion to the amount of taxable property owned by members of both societies.
> When this is done, the connection between Mr. Stearns and the First Congregational Society shall be dissolved.[32]

Samuel Gile closed the meeting with prayer. The whole town had attended, remaining until two o'clock on the morning of the twenty-eighth.

On March 4, the townsmen voted to relinquish all right, title, and interest in the bond held by the town or parish against Samuel Stearns, provided the First Parish would accept the recommendation of the council. This fulfilled the first requirement of the council.

The First Parish reported to the town that its members would accept the recommendation of the council "when they shall be possessed of adequate funds for settling with the Reverend Mr. Stearns."* [33]

From this time on, Mr. Stearns left the matter of his past salary in the hands of his attorney. He said there was a period after the council meeting when he received no salary at all. Late one evening when he was worrying about meeting his own responsibilities, there was a rap on his door. It was a messenger from a place five miles away with a hundred dollars in his hand. He said his wife's sister had just died. She had remembered the times when Samuel had helped her with religious advice, and she had asked that this money be given to him. The messenger said he had fifteen miles to ride that night, and he left immediately.

The Trinitarian Congregational Society was free of the town's tax funds and of the townsmen's vote in its affairs. None of the business of the Society was entered in the town clerk's book. It asked no help in building the meetinghouse; the members gave whatever they could, and it was enough.

Those who wanted a Unitarian Church in the old meetinghouse were not yet free. They asked how much money remained from the sale of pews and what was the annual income from the Page fund. They used these moneys to supply the pulpit and entertained guest speakers when they could. They wrote warrants for their business, attaching them to the town's warrants for meetings, and they transacted their business immediately after the town's was complete.

In the autumn of the next year, 1833, the Constitution of the Commonwealth of Massachusetts was amended to say that religious groups within the State had the power to raise money for their own expenses, to build houses for their worship services, and to pay their own ministers.

This legal action freed the Unitarians from the town. They established offices to carry on their business like those in the town, a parish committee, a treasurer, tax collectors, and a clerk. They drew up lists of inhabitants who they believed were interested in Unitarianism and met with each, asking for a subscription of money for a specified time. At last John Bacon, Unitarian treasurer, and the town's treasurer signed a statement that all the money had been separated, and the accounts were closed.

---

* It is not clear whether the members of the First Parish ever did have adequate funds for this purpose.

Fig. 46. The third meetinghouse in Bedford, 1832-33

As soon as his meetinghouse was completed, Samuel Stearns was installed as minister on June 5, 1833. (Fig. 46) On the next Sabbath, the twelfth, the first communion rite was to be observed there.

During the installation service, the trustees of the First Parish, Unitarian, called on Michael Crosby, senior deacon of Mr. Stearns's church, asking for the communion plate and the church records. As senior deacon, Mr. Crosby would have had the care of his church's property, but traditionally the records were kept by the minister, since he recorded vital statistics.

The ownership of property in cases where a church separated from a religious community, or parish, had been settled thirteen years before in the Massachusetts Supreme Court, the verdict being that the parish retained the property. The judge said he considered the feelings of those who had made gifts to their churches: if a person had attended public worship services and ordinances in a certain meetinghouse, he expected his gift to be used in that familiar setting, and not to be transported to an unknown place.[34]

Deacon Crosby promised the trustees of the First Parish that he would ask advice of his counsel, and if the plate and the records were to belong to the Unitarians, they should have them.

Perhaps many people knew that Widow Hannah (Merriam) Reed, daughter-in-law of John Reed, kept the communion silver in the house Nicholas Bowes had built. On Tuesday, the seventh, the trustees called on her to recover the communion service. Widow Reed felt she must have an order from Deacon Crosby before she should relinquish it.

The trustees obtained a writ of replevin for the property on Wednesday, the eighth. William Page, now a deacon of the First Parish, Unitarian, was to recover the parish property, and to have its care.

With the writ as a directive, Widow Reed gave the silver to Mr. Page. (Fig. 47) On Saturday evening she called on Mr. Stearns to tell him there was no communion service for the first communion rite the following day.

Early Sabbath morning Samuel, realizing that both his deacons lived far from the center of the town, rode to the home of Moses Hayward to see what could be done. The two men decided Moses would furnish a communion service. He opened his store, whose location is not known, and selected two large white pitchers, one

photograph courtesy Museum of Fine Arts, Boston

Fig. 47. The silver service of the First Parish of Bedford,
Unitarian-Universalist

From left to right: Beaker. 1738, Jacob Hurd, Boston (1702/3-1758), incribed: The Gift of/Dean Nath'l Meriam/ to the Church of Christ/ in BEDFORD/ with a legacy of L5/ from E. Taylor/ 1738; Beaker, Samuel Minott & William Simpkins, Boston (ca. 1770) inscribed: The Gift of Mrs. Susannah Dean/ to the Church of Christ in Bedford; Flagon, 1811, Jesse Churchill, Boston (1773-1819) inscribed within a wreath with acorns: PRESENTED/ to the/ CHURCH OF CHRIST/ in/ Bedford/ by/ Mrs. ANN PAGE/ AD 1811; Beaker, 1806, Joseph Loring, Boston (1743-1815), inscribed: The Gift of Mrs. Susanna Dean/ in part to the Church of Christ in/ BEDFORD; and Beaker, 1806, by Thomas Emery, of Boston (1781-1815), inscribed: The Property of the Church/ 1806/ of Christ in Bedford.

dozen white mugs, and two large white plates for the church to use for the ordinance. It was more than a year before the church had any other communion ware. When Widow Reed died six years later, she left the money for the principal part of a communion service to the Trinitarian Congregational Society.

Samuel said the Unitarians would have the records of the First Parish as soon as a copy had been made for the Trinitarians. To date, it has not been possible to discover either copy.

Samuel Stearns knew God had led his church through trials by raising up friends and benefactors. Looking around the new meetinghouse, he said, "Witness these lamps to enlighten the house of God, and this curtain which adorns the pulpit, and yonder accommodations of the choir . . . Witness, too, these seats, now filled with adoring worshippers; and these walls which have been erected by the free-will offerings of many and the princely bounties of some. And especially, and above all, witness this hallowed and commodious spot on whose fair bosom rests this sacred edifice . . ." [35] He was grateful that God had been so generous. On Thanksgiving day, November 28, 1833, he preached from Ps.116:6, 7: "I was brought low, and he helped me. Return unto thy rest, O my soul, for the Lord hath dealt bountifully with thee."

During the summer of 1834 the Reverend Samuel Stearns was able to preach only part of the time. He was now sixty-four and his cough, he wrote, was incessant and harassing. He continued as best he could until communion day, the first Sabbath in October. He arranged for one of his sons to conduct that service, and when it was over he entered the meetinghouse, taking his place at the communion table. He administered the ordinance for the last time, speaking briefly to his people. He closed the ceremony saying . . . "Be united, be prayerful, be steadfast, immovable, always abounding in the work of the Lord forasmuch as ye know that your labor is not in vain in the Lord." [36]

Samuel Stearns died on December 26, 1834. His funeral discourse was preached by the Reverend Samuel Sewall, of Burlington. Mr. Sewall said Samuel had once asked him to pray for him thus· "Pray not for my life, but pray that I may be patient and hold out to the end; pray that I may not be left to do anything which may bring dishonor upon religion or reproach upon my profession." [37]

The Reverend Samuel Stearns was buried on December 30, 1834, one hundred and four years after the church in Bedford was gathered. His body was placed in Vault Number 12 of the old burying place. It simply bore his name and that of his cousin, Elijah Stearns, who had died and been interred there three years before:

REV. S. STEARNS, E. STEARNS, ESQ.

❧ EPILOGUE ☙

This work has been a study of the causes of the rise of denominationalism in one small, homogeneous, New England town. After a hundred years of corporate life, the religious inhabitants separated into two churches following the congregational way, each choosing its covenant, its minister, and its theological philosophy.

Townsmen were no longer taxed for the maintenance of any church. Since the voluntary contributors were supporting two meetinghouses and two ministers, each church was poorer than the one had been before. It was to be forty years before members of another sect (Roman Catholic) were numerous enough to meet as a third church in the town.

The past was not well understood. What the people remembered was the continuous friction between the religious factions, the knowledge that the first three ministers had been dismissed, and that a split had occurred after the fourth had served conscientiously for more than thirty years. In the minds of the people, the movement was not associated with that in other New England towns, where parishes also separated into Trinitarian and Unitarian groups.

Here, churchmen began to speak of "our church" and "the other church." Because some did not agree with the property settlement, a feeling of injustice arose; fifty years after the schism, A. E. Brown pointed out: "The First Parish, and church connected with it, held the meetinghouse, all of the funds and communion silver, while the Trinitarian Congregational Society and associated church began their work with empty hands." * That same sense of injustice may not have disappeared even today.

---

* Abram English Brown, *History of Bedford,* p. 16.

No one remembered that it was the Reverend Samuel Stearns who would not accede to the direct request of the townsmen who paid his salary, and the reason why he could not accede was an intricate moral issue difficult to explain at the time and more difficult to recreate today.

In the First Parish, Unitarian, the distinction between a member of the church and a member of the parish was made for one hundred and twenty years (until the 1950's). At last, members of the church became "parishioners," members of the parish became "friends of the parish," and the Sunday audience was composed of "parishioners and friends."

Since 1950, several other denominations have arisen in the town. Some of these institutions were organized to serve an area far beyond the town bounds. Today, ties with the past are tenuous, and the epitaphs in the old burying place have become quaint. Once they spelled the tortuous way to religious freedom.

❧ APPENDICES ☙

APPENDIX I

Confession of Faith and Form of Covenant, to be assented to, by all persons, entering into fellowship with the Church of Christ in Bedford. By the Order of the Church, for the use of the Members.

Confession of Faith

You professedly believe there is one God, the Father, Son, and Holy Ghost; that the Bible is the word of God, which was written by the Prophets and Apostles, by the inspiration of the Holy Spirit. You believe the fall of man, the depravity of the human nature, and the redemption through mediation, intercession, and atonement of Christ;—that Christ hath appointed two special ordinances to be observed by every true believer, viz.—Baptism and the Lord's Supper;—that the qualifications for these ordinances are true repentance toward God, and faith toward our Lord Jesus Christ. You do also believe the future existence of the soul, the resurrection of the body, and a day of future judgment, in which, every one will receive a reward according to his works.

Do you profess thus to believe?

The Covenant

You do now, humbly and penitently, asking the forgiveness of all your sins, through the blood of the great Redeemer, give up yourself to God, in an everlasting covenant, in our Lord Jesus Christ. And, as in the presence of God, angels, and men, you do solemnly promise, that, by the assistance of the Divine Spirit, you will forsake the vanities of this present evil world, and approve yourself a true disciple of Jesus Christ, in all good carriage toward God, and toward man. And you likewise promise, so long as God shall continue you among us, to walk in communion with the Church of Christ in this place; and, as opportunity shall offer, in love to watch over other professing Christians among us; and to submit to the power and discipline of Christ in his Church, and duly to attend the seals, censures, or whatever ordinance Christ has commanded to be observed by his people, so far as the Lord, by his Word and Spirit, has, or shall reveal to you, to be your duty; adoring the doctrine of God our Savior in all things, and avoiding the appearance of evil.

And by daily prayer to God, in the name of Christ, you will endeavor to seek for grace to enable you to keep this Covenant.

Do you thus promise?

I then, as ministering in holy things in this place, declare you to be a member in full communion with the visible Church of Christ. And in the name of the Church here, I promise, by the assistance of the Divine Spirit, we will carry it toward you, as toward a member of the same body with ourselves; watching over you, and that for your good, with a spirit of meekness, tenderness, and love; earnestly praying, that Jesus Christ, the great Head of the Church, would delight to dwell among us, and bless us, and that both we and you may obtain mercy of the Lord, to be faithful in his Covenant, and glorify him with that holiness, which becometh his house forever.

Amen.

APPENDIX II

*Will of Anna Page**

I, Anna Page, widow and relict of Thomas Page, late of Bedford, in the County of Middlesex and Commonwealth of Massachusetts, Yeoman, deceased . . . I humbly commit and commend my soul to God my Creator, in and through Jesus Christ my Redeemer, whose righteousness and grace are all my hope for pardon and eternal salvation. My Body I recommend to a Christian burial at the discretion of my Executor in the blessed hope of a joyful resurrection at the last day . . .

Taking into consideration the vast importance and necessity of supporting the Gospel ministry, it is my will that after my Executor shall have paid all the foregoing leagacys [*sic*]—all debts, bills of cost and charges of every kind—all, the remainder of my estate of any kind and wherever found, be appropriated to that use, and accordingly I do hereby give and bequeath said remainder to the town of Bedford as a fund to aid in the support of the Gospel ministry, to be disposed of in the manner following. That is to say: The capital of the fund shall be put and always kept at interest, upon good security—with sufficient sureties for the same. One-sixth part of the income arising therefrom shall be annually added to the principal as an increasing fund forever—the other five-sixths parts of the annual income to be appropriated annually in aid of the support of the Gospel ministry in the present standing order or congregational order forever, and no part of said fund shall ever be appropriated in aid or support of any other than the present standing congregational order forever, and no part of the said fund shall ever be appropriated in aid of any suit at law or any contention whatever, and my will further is, that three persons, all belonging to the church, shall be

---

* From Abram English Brown, *History of the Town of Bedford, op. cit.*, p. 15.

annually chosen by the town as a committee to take care of the said
fund, and that a Book shall be kept by the town clerk, for the time being
in which shall be fairly entered this clause in my will and also the capital
of the fund and the annual income thereof together with the annual ap-
propriations and expenditures of said income, to be kept open for the
perusal of all persons therein concerned forever—but my will further is,
that whenever the income of the said fund shall be more than sufficient
for the support of the Gospel ministry in Bedford, the remainder of the
income of said fund shall be appropriated to support the Poor, Teaching
Sacred Music, and the support of Schools or Public buildings, and my
will further is, the said sum, whatever it may be found to be, shall be
paid by my Executor to the committee to be chosen for the above purpose, in two years after my decease, and a true report of the said fund,
with the annual appropriation and expenditure thereof, shall be annually
made to the town by the Committee having the care of the same forever,
which report shall be recorded by the town clerk in the Book which is
kept by him for that purpose forever.

Dated, signed and sealed, February twenty-third, 1810.

Anna Page

APPENDIX III

*Catalogue of Church Members, 1821 (Female)
During the Ministry of Samuel Stearns*

Abbott, Sarah, probably descended from the first covenantor, Obed
Blake, Hulda, unknown
Bowers, Martha, née Porter, whose family had moved to Bedford about
  1760
Buttrick, Mary, wife of Willard
Clark, Ruth, daughter of Ebenezer, who moved to Bedford from Brain-
  tree after the Revolution
Crosby, Lucy, wife of Deacon Michael Crosby
Davis, Allice, née Abbott, great-granddaughter of the first covenantor,
  Obed
Davis, Martha, née Skinner, wife of Eleazer
Fassett, Sarah, probably descended from Josiah Fassett
Fitch, Lydia, née Smith, of Waltham, widow, sister-in-law of Deacon
  Moses Fitch
Fitch, Mary, née Fowle, of Woburn, widow, whose husband had been
  Deacon Moses' cousin
Gleason, Lydia, wife of Joel
Hadley, Lucy, unknown
Hartwell, Desire, wife of Samuel
Hartwell, Elizabeth, née Mead, aunt of Amos and Benjamin F.
Hartwell, Mary, née Lake, widow, stepmother of Amos and Benjamin F.
Hartwell, Sarah, née Reed, distantly related to Amos and Benjamin F.
Hayward, Lucy, née Page, great-granddaughter of the first covenantor,
  Nathaniel, wife of Mather
Hayward, Sarah, née Lane, great-granddaughter of Deacon Job, wife of
  Ebenezer, of Acton
Hill, Susan, née Bacon, perhaps great-granddaughter of Deacon Benjamin
Hosmer, Ruth, listed twice: she was Ruth Clark, above

Jones, Rebecca, wife of John
Lane, Allice, née Stearns, cousin of the minister
Lane, Amelia, wife of Josiah Stearns Lane, nephew of the minister
Lane, Arinda, granddaughter of the first covenantor, John
Lane, Fanny (Fanna), granddaughter of Deacon Job
Lane, Hannah, perhaps sister of Arinda, although there were other Han-
    nahs
Lane, Hannah, great-granddaughter of Deacon Job through Luke or
    Ziba; or mother of Hannah and Arinda
Lane, Phoebe, granddaughter of the first covenantor, John; sister or aunt
    of Hannah
Lane, Ruhamah, née Page, great-granddaughter of the first covenantor,
    Nathaniel
Lane, Sarah, née Stearns, sister of the minister
Lawrence, Dorcas, unknown
May, Betsey, unknown, but later married Joshua Page
Mead, Abigail, wife of Asa Mead
Merriam, Hannah, née Brooks, of Lincoln, widow, had married John,
    grandson of Deacon Nathaniel
Merriam, Lucy, sister of Jonas
Page, Clariot, great-great-granddaughter of the first covenantor, Na-
    thaniel
Page, Elizabeth, great-great-granddaugter of the first covenantor, Na-
    thaniel
Page, Lucy, née Simonds, wife of William
Page, Sarah, née Brown, widow, grandmother of Elizabeth Page
Parkhurst, Anna, née Lane, niece of the minister
Pollard, Jane, descended from Oliver
Porter, Rebecca, née Page, great-granddaughter of the first covenantor,
    Nathaniel
Preston, Ruhamah, née Lane, great-granddaughter of the first covenantor,
    John, wife of Amariah
Putnam, Hannah, née Evans, niece of Mrs. Desire Hartwell
Reed, Hannah, née Merriam, great-granddaughter of Deacon Nathaniel,
    widow and daughter-in-law of John Reed, Esq.
Reed, Sarah, née Webber, daughter of John and Sarah (Fassett)
Simonds, Amattai, née Webber, niece of Sarah Reed, wife of Zebedee
Simonds, Elizabeth, second wife of Benjamin, Jr.
Skelton, Iza, née Bacon, daughter of Oliver, married Dr. Benjamin, of
    Reading
Skelton, Keziah, wife or mother of Daze; the family moved to Bedford
    from Woburn
Spaulding, Susanna, wife of Sampson
Stearns, Abigail, wife of the minister
Stearns, Betsey, née Davis, daughter of Deacon Thaddeus Davis
Stearns, Elizabeth, sister of the minister, wife of Elijah

Stearns, Mary, sister of the minister
Stearns, Sally, née Cole, sister-in-law of Abner and Elijah
Webber, Bethiah, née Lane, granddaughter of Deacon Job; wife of John
Webber, Hannah, née Davis, daughter of Deacon Stephen; wife of James
Webber, Susanna, née Simonds, mother of James, John, and William
Wilson, Elizabeth, wife or daughter of Francis
Wilson, Sarah, unknown
Woods, Mary, unknown
Wright, Dorcas, wife of James, Jr., who was the son of Deacon James Wright
Wright, Ruth, widow of Deacon James; probably born Ruth Fassett

APPENDIX IV

*Catalogue of Church Members, 1821 (Male)
During the Ministry of Samuel Stearns*

Stearns, Samuel, Pastor
Crosby, Michael, Deacon, who had moved to Bedford from Billerica
Fitch, Moses, Deacon, grandson of first covenantor, Samuel; husband of
    minister's cousin

Bacon, Benjamin, grandson of Deacon Benjamin
Bacon, Elijah, son of Benjamin
Buttrick, Willard, who had moved to Bedford from Concord about 1800
Davis, Eleazer, great-grandson of the first covenantor, Eleazer
Fiske, Isaac, unknown
Hartwell, Amos, great-grandson of the first covenantor, William; later to
    be named a deacon
Hartwell, Benjamin F., brother of Amos
Hartwell, Samuel, grandson of the first covenantor, William
Hayward, Ebenezer, of Acton, husband of Sarah Lane
Hayward, Mather, husband of Lucy Page
Hill, Joseph, son or brother of Josiah
Hill, Josiah, father or brother of Joseph
Hutchinson, James, unknown
Jones, John, probably son of Lieutenant Timothy Jones
Kinsman, Timothy, husband of Lucy Abbott, great-granddaughter of
    Obed
Lane, Jonathan, great-grandson of the first covenantor, John
Mead, Asa, great-grandson of Ruth Taylor Mead Cheever, wife of the
    first covenantor, Daniel
Merriam, Jonas, great-grandson of Deacon Nathaniel's brother, Samuel

188

Page, Christopher, great-grandson of the first covenantor, Nathaniel
Page, Moses, great-grandson of the first covenantor, Nathaniel, cousin of Christopher
Page, William, brother of Moses
Pearce, Thomas, unknown
Preston, Amariah, husband of Ruhamah Lane, great-granddaughter of the first covenantor, John
Reed, David, distantly related to John, Esq.
Reed, John, son of David or of John, Esq.
Reed, Josiah (Jesse?), distantly related to David and John, Esq.
Simonds, Benjamin, Jr., moved to Bedford from Woburn in 1805
Simonds, John, son of Zebedee
Simonds, Zebedee, brother of Benjamin, Jr.; later to be named deacon
Spaulding, Sampson, lived in Billerica but came to Bedford for worship services
Stearns, Abner, cousin of the minister
Stearns, Elijah, brother of Abner
Stearns, Samuel H., son of the minister
Stearns, William, cousin of the minister; husband of Betsey Davis, granddaughter of Deacon Stephen
Webber, James, son of John and Sarah (Fassett) Webber
Webber, John, brother of James
Webber, William, brother of James

APPENDIX V

Polls compared to church members in 1821

Polls in Bedford	Member of Church	Number of Pews
	Sarah Abbott	
Moses Abbott		
Oliver Abbott		
Za——iel Adams		
Benjamin Bacon	Benjamin Bacon	
Benjamin Bacon, Jr.		1
Elijah Bacon	Elijah Bacon	1
John Bacon		
Reuben Bacon		
(Sarah Bacon)		
Thompson Bacon		1
Thompson Bacon, Jr.		
	Hulda Blake	
Simon Blodgett		1
Bradley Bowers		
	Martha Bowers	
Joseph Brown		1
Samuel Butler		
Daniel Butters		
Franklin Butters		
	Mary Buttrick	
Willard Buttrick	Willard Buttrick	1
Benjamin Clark		
James Clark		
	Ruth Clark	

Polls in Bedford	Member of Church	Number of Pews
John Colburn		
	Lucy Crosby	
Michael Crosby, Deacon	Michael Crosby, Deacon	4
Daniel Cumings		
Leonard Cutler		
Emery Darby		
	Allice Davis	
Eleazer Davis		
	Eleazer Davis, Jr.	1
	Martha Davis	
Thaddeus Davis		
Thomas Dean		
John Dudley		
Silas Dudley		
Silas Farrer		
	Sarah Fassett	
	Isaac Fiske	
Alford Fitch		1
David Fitch		2
(Heirs of Jeremiah Fitch)		
		Jeremiah Fitch, 3
Joel Fitch		1
John Fitch		
Joseph Fitch		
	Lydia Fitch	
(Heirs of Mary Fitch)		
	Mary Fitch	
Moses Fitch, Deacon	Moses Fitch, Deacon	1
Moses Fitch, Jr.		1
Charles Gleason		
Joel Gleason	Lydia Gleason	
William Goodridge		1
Uriah Goodwin		
Jacob Gragg		
Abel Green		
Reuben Green		
	Lucy Hadley	
John Hardy		
Solomon Harrington		
Amos Hartwell	Amos Hartwell	
Benjamin Hartwell	Benjamin Hartwell	
	Desire Hartwell	
	Elizabeth Hartwell	

Polls in Bedford	Member of Church	Number of Pews
Joseph Hartwell		
(Mary Hartwell, widow)	Mary Hartwell, widow	
Samuel Hartwell	Samuel Hartwell	
	Sarah Hartwell	
William Hartwell		1
	Ebenezer Hayward	
	Lucy Hayward	
Mather Hayward	Mather Hayward	2
	Sarah Hayward	
	Joseph Hill	
Josiah Hill	Josiah Hill	1
	Susan Hill	
Stephen Hooker		
Castilio Hosmer		
Gustavus Hosmer		
Leander Hosmer		
	Ruth Hosmer	
Hezekiah Hutchinson		
	James Hutchinson	
	John Jones	1
	Rebecca Jones	
Timothy Jones		1
George Kelly		
John Kendall		
	Timothy Kinsman	
	Allice Lane	
	Amelia Lane	
	Arinda Lane	
David Lane		1
David Lane, Jr.		
Eliab Lane		1
	Fanna Lane	
	Hannah Lane	
James Lane		
(Mrs. Jonathan Lane, Hannah)	Hannah Lane	
		Job Lane, 1
Jonathan Lane	Jonathan Lane	1
Luke Lane		
Oliver Lane		
	Phoebe Lane	
Roger Lane		1
	Ruhamah Lane	
Samuel Lane		
	Sarah Lane	
Seth Lane		

Polls in Bedford	Member of Church	Number of Pews
Solomon Lane		1
Stephen Lane		1
	Dorcas Lawrence	
	Betsey May	
	Abigail Mead	
Jabez Marble		
Asa Mead	Asa Mead	1
(Hannah Merriam, widow)	Hannah Merriam, widow	
John Merriam		2
	Jonas Merriam	
	Lucy Merriam	
Christopher Page	Christopher Page	
	Clariot Page	
	Elizabeth Page	
Joshua Page		2
	Lucy Page	
Moses Page	Moses Page	1
Nathaniel Page, Jr.		1
	Sarah Page	
Timothy Page		
William Page	William Page	
	Anna Parkhurst	
	Thomas Pearce	
(Elizabeth Pollard, widow)		
	Jane Pollard	
Obed Pollard		1
Oliver Pollard		1
Oliver Pollard, Jr.		
Asa Porter		
	Rebecca Porter	
William Porter		
Amariah Preston, Dr.	Amariah Preston, Dr.	1
	Ruhamah Preston	
	David Price, 1	
	Hannah Putnam	
	Jonas Putnam, 1	
Asa Reed		
Benjamin Reed		
David Reed	David Reed	3
David Reed, Jr.		1
	Hannah Reed	
Isaac Reed		
Jesse Reed		
John Reed	John Reed	3
John Reed, Captain		1
	Josiah Reed	

Polls in Bedford	*Member of Church*	*Number of Pews*
Oliver Reed		
Otis Reed		
Roger Reed		
	Sarah Reed	
David Rice		
Jesse Robinson		1
Jesse Robinson, Jr.		
Benjamin Russell		
Samuel Sage		1
Abel Shed		
	Amattai Simonds	
	Benjamin Simonds,	½
Benjamin Simonds, Jr.	Benjamin Simonds, Jr.	2
	Elizabeth Simonds	
John Simonds	John Simonds	
Moses Simonds		
Zebedee Simonds, Deacon	Zebedee Simonds, Deacon	1½
Artemus Skelton		
Daze Skelton		1
Elijah Skelton		2
Horace Skelton		
	Iza Skelton	
	Keziah Skelton	
Lendall Skelton		
Loel Skelton		
Leonard Spaulding		
	Sampson Spaulding	1
	Susanna Spaulding	
Loel Sprague		1
	Abigail Stearns	
	Abner Stearns	
	Betsey Stearns	
David Stearns		
Elijah Stearns	Elijah Stearns	1
	Elizabeth Stearns	
	Mary Stearns	
	Sally Stearns	
	Samuel Stearns, Rev. Mr.	town's pew
	Samuel H. Stearns	
Simeon Stearns		1
William Stearns	William Stearns	
Thomas Temple		
Elijah Watson		

		Number of
Polls in Bedford	*Member of Church*	*Pews*
	Bethiah Webber	
	Hannah Webber	
Hiram Webber		
James Webber	James Webber	1
John Webber	John Webber	1
(Susanna Webber, widow)	Susanna Webber, widow	
Thomas Webber		
William Webber	William Webber	1
Isaac Weston		
Abner Wheeler		
Howard Willis		
William Willis		
	Elizabeth Wilson	
Francis Wilson		
Joseph Wilson		
Levi Wilson		1
	Sarah Wilson	
	Mary Woods	
	Dorcas Wright	
James Wright		1
Joel Wright		
	Ruth Wright	
Francis Yates		
(Widow Vila)		

APPENDIX VI

Descendants of the original covenantor, Job Lane, who were members of the church in 1821:

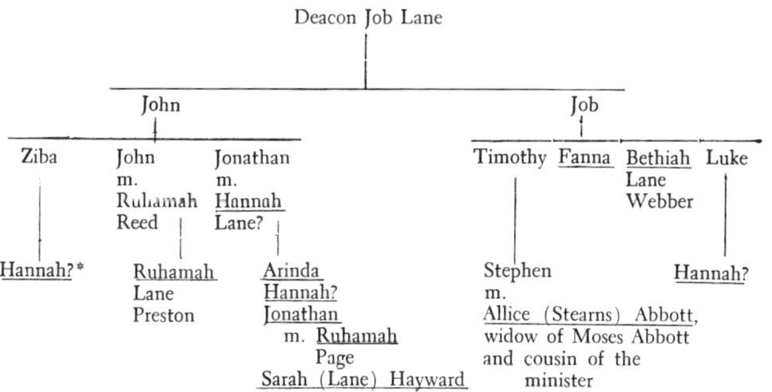

APPENDIX VII

Descendants of the original pew owner, James Lane, who were members of the church in 1821:

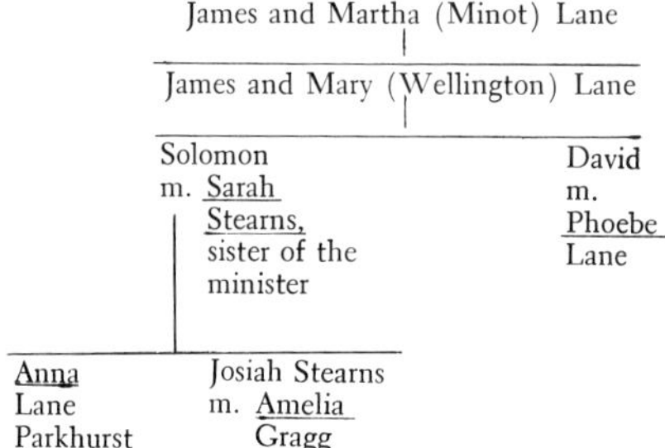

APPENDIX VIII

Descendants of Colonal John Lane who were members of the church in 1821:

* There were only two persons named Hannah Lane who were members.
Underlined name indicates membership.

NOTES

NOTES

I. *The Place, the People, and the Church*

1. There were few roads in South Billerica and Concord East Part. A main or country road, planned in 1660, ran from Billerica meetinghouse to Concord meetinghouse. (See Henry A. Hazen, *History of Billerica*, p. 89; Brown, *History of Bedford*, p. 34.) Brown believed its course was moved at one time to higher ground. It was traced in dotted lines on "Proposed Zoning By-Law and Map," Bedford Planning Board, November, 1958. Today it has several names. It is Bedford Road in Billerica; North Road in Bedford; a forgotten trail through Cedar or Sancto Domingo Swamp; route 62 in Bedford and Concord; Old Bedford Road in Concord, and route 2a in Concord.

The Bacon family was living near the Shawsheen River by or before 1680, and a way was laid from their mill north to Billerica meetinghouse. This has become Old Billerica Road.

By 1721 a road led from Woburn westward along Vine Brook, passing near Bacon's mill, and crossing the hills until it met the Concord-Billerica road. (See Hazen, *op. cit.*, pp. 95, 198–99.) Today most of it is Pine Hill Road. At about the same time, this road was connected more directly to Concord by laying what is now Brooksbie Road and a part of the Great Road north of the town line. The inhabitants called this the road from Concord to Woburn. (See Registry of Deeds for Middlesex County, South, Book 31, p. 215.)

The present Shawsheen Road ran directly to the town line to reach one family whose house was almost on the town line.

Virginia Road in Concord was the old way to the Bay (Boston). Concord East Part families lived along it, and by 1721 they had spread into the meadowland. Consequently a road was laid from Bay Way to Shawsheen Corner, where Lexington, Billerica, and Concord met near the river. It drifted across the meadows and when it did not reach a home

directly, a private road, called a lane or way and often equipped with a
set of bars, led from it to the house. (See Concord town records, 12/26/
1705, and 8/9/1721.) A portion of the drift way was represented by
Brown in his frontispiece map, but he included roads laid after Bedford
was incorporated in 1729. Today, most of the area is occupied by facilities
at Hanscom Air Field.

Other private lanes may have been in use as well as the rumored
way, remembered by an elderly inhabitant as being open as late as 1910.
(See map 3.)

2. Those living in Concord East Part in 1711–12 who were to become important in Bedford Church were:

Cheever, Daniel, who was 17 in 1711
Colburn, Benjamin, who was probably in his early 30's
Davis, Daniel, 38
Davis, Eleazer, Jr., 5
Davis, Stephen, 25
Dean, Joseph, 44
Fassett, John, 41
French, Jonathan, 21
French, Joseph, 62 (from tombstone)
Hartwell, John, 38
Hartwell, William, Sr., 40
Hartwell, William, Jr., 8
Merriam, John, 7
Merriam, Nathaniel, 39
Merriam, Samuel, 30
Stearns, Zachariah, 9
Taylor, David, 9
Wheeler, James, 9
Wheeler, Richard, probably about 15
Woolley, Thomas, 13.

3. For a thorough discussion of the Congregational Way in the
Bay Colony, see Ezra Hoyt Byington, *The Puritan*; Williston Walker,
A History of the Congregational Churches in the United States; Perry
Miller, *Errand Into the Wilderness*, and *The New England Mind From
Colony to Province.*

4. There is no list of the townsmen of Bedford at the time of its incorporation. The following names have been gathered from three sources:
those who signed the petition to leave Concord, an incomplete list of
those who asked to leave Billerica, and those who are mentioned in the
earliest records of the church and town of Bedford. Those who had lived
in Billerica were:

Abbott, Obed, a weaver who, as a bridegroom, bought a farm in
Billerica in 1725

Bacon, Jonathan, born in Billerica, who bought his father's mill on the Shawsheen River in 1700

Bacon, Joseph, brother of Jonathan, who sold his property on Shawsheen River and bought a farm in Concord East Part, 1719–20

Bacon, Josiah, nephew and neighbor of Jonathan

Fassett, Josiah, who had inherited his father's farm, brother of John, of Concord East Part, and Joseph, of Lexington

Fitch, John, son of Samuel (below)

Fitch, Joseph, son of Samuel (below)

Fitch, Samuel, whose father had married Sarah Lane and had been given part of the Lane property, which Samuel inherited

Kendall, Jacob, who had raised a large family in Billerica

Kidder, Benjamin, a bridegroom of Billerica who was moving into the South Part

Lane, James, whose grandfather had bought the Winthrop farm and who was sharing it (*see* Brown, *op. cit.*, pp. 6, 7)

Lane, Job, brother of James, sharing Winthrop farm

Lane, Mr. Job, called "Mr." to distinguish him from his relative, Job

Lane, John, brother of James, sharing Winthrop farm

Page, Christopher, son of Nathaniel (below)

Page, John, son of Nathaniel (below)

Page, Nathaniel, whose father had bought a farm in 1688 which Nathaniel inherited

Putnam, Israel, a bridegroom from Salem Village who married Sarah Bacon, daughter of Jonathan, and bought a farm near his wife's family

Simonds, William, about whom nothing is known; perhaps an absentee landowner

Whipple, John, probably related to Susanna (Whipple) Lane, mother of James, Job, and John (above)

Wilkins, John, about whom nothing is known

Wilson, John, whose father had a mill on Vine Brook which he inherited.

Those who lived in Concord East Part were:

Cheever, Daniel, born in Cambridge, moved to Concord East Part as a young man, probably to be with or near his aunt, Mary (Cheever) Taylor; married Ruth (Taylor) Mead and had her late husband's farm near the Taylors

Colburn, Benjamin, whose birthplace is unknown, but who had married Elizabeth French of Concord East Part and lived near her parents. See Joseph (below)

Davis, Daniel, who shared the Davis property which his grandfather and his father had acquired

Davis, Eleazer, nephew and neighbor of Daniel
Davis, Joseph, probably son of Daniel
Davis, Stephen, brother of Daniel
Dean, Joseph, who shared property his father had acquired in 1663
Fassett, John, born in Billerica and living in Concord East Part on property given to his wife
French, Jonathan, son of Joseph (below)
French, Joseph, who had owned a farm in Concord East Part since 1680
Hartwell, John, brother of William (below)
Hartwell, William, Sr., who shared his grandfather's farm
Hartwell, William, Jr., son of William (above)
Merriam, John, son of Nathaniel (below)
Merriam, Nathaniel, who shared his grandfather's and his father's farm
Stearns, Zachariah, whose father had married Mercy Davis of Concord, and who lived near a Davis family
Taylor, David, nephew of Mary (Cheever) Taylor and through her, cousin of Daniel Cheever (above)
Watkins, Andrew, birthplace unknown; he owned land in Concord East Part for a time and sold to move to Marlborough; perhaps a speculator
Wheeler, James, probably sharing land which had been in his family since 1663
Wheeler, Richard, probably cousin of James (above), who married Jemime French and lived near the Joseph French family
Woolley, Thomas, whose father had married Rebecca French and had lived near her family
Additionally, there was Dinsmore, Thomas, who had seven children born in Bedford before he moved away. His origin is unknown, but the name reappears at Swan Island, Maine, in 1770 (*see* Henry Sewall Webster, *Silvester Gardiner*, p. 20). Perhaps he was a speculator or fortune seeker.

5. This version of the petition is from Lemuel Shattuck's *History of the Town of Concord*, pp. 255–56.
6. Brown, *op. cit.*, pp. 77–81.

II. *Reverend Mr. Nicholas Bowes*

1. By selecting the center of the town, Bedford founders deliberately avoided discussion and dissension as to the location of the meetinghouse. Such was not the case in neighboring towns, for example, Harvard and Watertown, where anger flared and it became difficult to "appease a broil" as to where to set the meetinghouse. (*See* Ola Elizabeth Winslow,

Meetinghouse Hill, pp. 118–26.) In Harvard, where an impasse occurred, the General Court was called on to "stick the stake" and thus pick the site. At the dead of night the stake was often removed or moved to a different position. Even after the spot had been picked and the frame erected, the opposition sometimes pulled down the frame after dark.

2. Hazen, *op. cit.*, pp. 210–12, described a strip of common land, given by the town to Samuel Hill in 1707, as being part of what is now the center of Bedford. It lay on the south side of the road from Concord to Woburn and extended southward to the old town line. By 1730, when Bedford had been organized, that strip had been subdivided among various owners into ten pieces. The diagram below shows the relative position of the land where the meetinghouse was built (Registry of Deeds for Middlesex County, North).

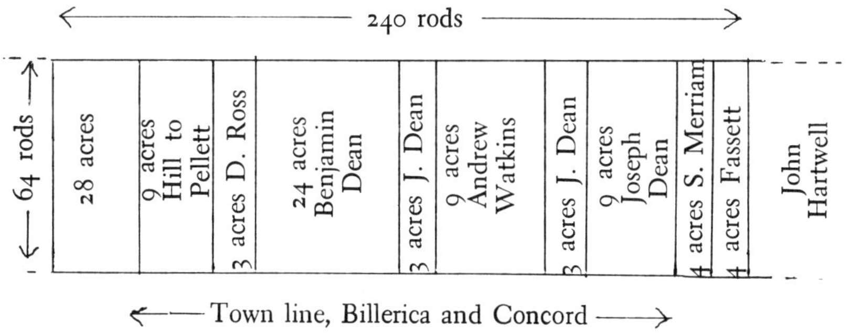

240 rods

64 rods

28 acres · 9 acres Hill to Pellett · 3 acres D. Ross · 24 acres Benjamin Dean · 3 acres J. Dean · 9 acres Andrew Watkins · 3 acres J. Dean · 9 acres Joseph Dean · 4 acres S. Merriam · 4 acres Fassett · John Hartwell

Town line, Billerica and Concord

3. Registry of Deeds, South, *op. cit. Book* 31, p. 215.

4. Brown, *op. cit.*, p. 54.

5. Lucius R. Paige, *History of Cambridge*, pp. 507, 572. The two families had actually touched in marriage when Ebenezer's cousin, Tabitha Hancock, and Nicholas's cousin, Daniel Champney, had wed. Nicholas knew the oldest son, John Hancock, who was a librarian at the college.

6. Shattuck, *op. cit.*, pp. 262–63.

7. Winslow, *op. cit.*, pp. 22–26; and Walker, *op. cit.*, p. 104.

8. Shattuck, *op. cit.*, pp 262–63.

9. Winslow, *op. cit.*, p. 29, says that to the 17th century Englishman, church member or not, life on this earth had eternal consequences, and he lived out his life in that unquestioned conviction. Sermons by "sound learned godly" ministers offered the best means at hand to solve the riddle of life. A town needed a minister as it needed a blacksmith.

10. Robert S. Pope, *The Half-Way Covenant*, pp. 13–46.

11.

Townsman	*Office*	*Dates when elected*
Bacon, Joseph	tithingman	
Bacon, Josiah	constable	
Colburn, Benjamin	fielddriver	
Dean, Joseph	sealer of leather	
French, Jonathan	fenceviewer	
Merriam, John	hogreeve	March 2, 1729–30
Merriam, Samuel	treasurer	
Page, John	hogreeve	
Whipple, John	surveyor of highways	
Woolley, Thomas	surveyor of highways	
Davis, Joseph	constable	November 18, 1729
Stearns, John	fenceviewer	March 1, 1730–31
Wilson, Francis	tithingman	
Crosby, Thomas	constable	March 6, 1731–32
Fassett, John	selectman	
Hartwell, Isaac	tythingman	
Grimes, William	constable	March 5, 1732–33
Raymond, Paul	selectman	
Fitch, Joseph	builder of the meetinghosue	9/22/1730
Lane, James	seated in the meetinghouse	10/18/1734
Lane, Job, Sr.	a resident (according to Brown, *op. cit.*, p. 98)	
Simonds, William	not excused from ministerial rate	10/13/1729
Wilson, John	noted in Brown, *op. cit.*, geneal. sec., p. 44.	

The hyphenated dates are from the Julian calendar which was in use until 1753. The months of various lengths were identical to those of today. The New Year commenced on March 21, and dates between Jaunary 1 and March 21 carried the figures for the old year which was waning and the new year which was approaching. Ten days were lost when the calendar was changed to the Gregorian in October 1752.

12. Charles Hudson, *History of Lexington*, I, 313.

13. Bedford town records, 1/7/1730–31.

14. All the pew lots were described in Bedford town records, 10/18 and 12/26, 1734.

15. Brown, *op. cit.*, p. 23.

16. Bedford town records, 12/26/1734.

17. *Ibid.*, from 5/14/1733 to 12/7/1734.

18. These were not the first deaths of original covenantors. Joseph French died in 1732 (Brown, *op. cit.*, p. 84); Daniel Cheever, in 1733, and Jacob Kendall, probably in 1737 (Bedford Vital Statistics).

19. Eunice Taylor, wife of John, of Concord, took an unusual interest in Bedford Church because she had three daughters whose families had parts in the organization of the town and the gathering of the church. They were:

Unice, born 10/22/78; m. Samuel Fitch, after 1716
Mary, born 2/21/81; m. Nathaniel Merriam, in 1707
Rebecka, born 6/27/87; m. Joseph Bacon, in 1716
In addition, the first covenantor David Taylor was Eunice's nephew through her husband's brother, Abraham. Shortly after Bedford held its first thanksgiving, Nov. 12, 1730, the "good people of Concord contributed for the use of the church in Bedford £6," and Widow Eunice Taylor, Widow Sarah Bateman, and Isaac Stearns gave 10 shillings each. Deacon Merriam left a legacy of £6 to the church, which meant £11 could be spent on the communion cup (Shattuck, *op. cit.*, p. 264).

The communion silver is in the care of the Musem of Fine Arts, Boston, Massachusetts.

20. For a detailed study of the Great Awakening, see Edwin Scott Gaustad, *The Great Awakening in New England*.

21. John Gillies, *Memoirs of Reverend George Whitefield*, p. 422.

22. *Ibid.*, p. 34.

23. Samuel Eliot Morison, *Three Centuries of Harvard*, p. 85. Tillotson (1630–1694) was the Archbishop of Canterbury from 1691 to 1694 (*see* Bridgewater and Kurtz, *Columbia Encyclopedia*, p. 2139, col. 1). Samuel Clarke (1675–1729) was an English divine and philosopher whose *The Scripture Doctrine of Unity* appeared in 1712. (Among other pulpits, Clarke had St. James, Westminster.) John Clarke had his sermons printed in London in 1730 (*See Columbia Encyclopedia*, p. 428, col. 3.)

24. Paige, *op. cit.*, p. 293.

25. Shattuck, *op. cit.*, p. 167.

26. George L. Clark, *A History of Connecticut*, p. 267ff. Two versions of Nathan Cole's report of his trip to hear George Whitefield exist in the Connecticut Historical Society, Hartford, Connecticut, as pointed out by Leonard W. Larrabee (*William and Mary Quarterly*, 3rd. ser., vii (1950), 588–91). The original version is used here, with permission of the Connecticut Historical Society, for Nathan's ride to the meeting; the second or corrected version, for his reaction to the sermon and for the fact that he considered himself an Arminian. As Larrabee points out in a footnote, some authors have paraphrased portions of Cole's journal.

27. Shattuck, *op. cit.*, pp. 167–79.

28. Paige, *op. cit.*, p. 294.

29. Clifford K. Shipton, *Harvard Graduates*, VII, 256.

30. Hudson, *op. cit.*, I, 314, 316.

31. Bedford town records, 3/5/1753. The description of all the pew lots was entered at the same time.

32. *Status of the founding families:*
Abbott: died in Bedford, 1773; his family continued there.
Bacon: the name is in Bedford now.
Cheever: died in Bedford in 1733; the name disappeared.

Davis: the name is in Bedford now.

Dinsmore: disappeared about 1736; said to have moved to New Hampshire.

Fassett: the name was here until 1771 (*see* Brown, *op. cit.*, genealogical section, p. 10).

Fitch: the name is in Bedford now.

French: sold out to Woolley (*see* Brown, *op. cit.*, p. 105), and the family disappeared.

Hartwell: the name was here until this century.

Kendall: disappeared about 1740.

Kidder: disappeared about 1755; may have moved to Marlborough.

Lane: the name was here until 1950.

Merriam: the name was here until the 1850's (*see* Brown, *op. cit.*, genealogical section, p. 25).

Page: the name was here as late as the 1890's (*see ibid*, p. 27).

Putnam: moved away in 1784; he went to Chelmsford (Registry of Deeds, South, *op. cit.*, Book 88, p. 70).

Taylor: disappeared about 1750.

Wheeler: James moved to New Hampshire; Richard disappeared about 1750.

Necrology of the original pew owners:

Bacon, Josiah, died before 1751	Lane, James, died in 1783
Bacon, Joseph, died in 1747	Lane, Job, died in 1762
Colburn, Benjamin, died in 1746	Lane, John, died in 1763
Davis, Daniel, died in 1741	Merriam, Nathaniel, died in 1738
Davis, Stephen, died in 1738	Page, Nathaniel, died in 1755
Fassett, John, died in 1736–37	Woolley, Thomas, not known
Hartwell, William, died in 1742	

33. See Note 24.

34. See Note 26.

35. Daniel, of Littleton, son of Daniel, who was son of John and Elizabeth

Daniel, of Exeter, son of John, who was son of John and Elizabeth

Nathaniel, of Ipswich, son of John, who was son of John and Elizabeth

Nathaniel, of Portsmouth, son of John and Elizabeth

John, of Eliot and Kittery, son of John, who was son of John and Elizabeth

John, of Ipswich, son of John and Elizabeth

An uncle of Daniel, of Littleton, John, and a cousin Nathaniel shared the pulpit in Ipswich as colleagues; his cousin John was preaching in Eliot and Kittery (now Maine); his cousin Daniel was the first minister in the second church in Exeter, New Hampshire; and his deceased uncle Nathaniel had had the pulpit in Portsmouth, New Hampshire, until his untimely death.

There were two Old Light pulpits in Newbury, a town adjacent to Daniel Rogers' home town of Ipswich, that of the Reverend John Lowell in Newburyport, in the Third Parish on the south bank of the Parker River, and that of the Reverend Christopher Toppan, in the First or original Parish, a mile or so to the southeast on the estuary of the same river.

George Whitefield had preached in Newbury in 1740, and religious differences had been smoldering among the inhabitants ever since his visit. Revival meetings broke out in York in 1741, and the people of Newbury and Ipswich were kept up to date on the happenings there as the Reverend Samuel Moody of York was a son of a Newbury family. Dissension between the New Lights and the Old Lights increased until the New Lights were so numerous that they began to search for ways to have New Light preaching for themselves.

In 1742, two cousins of the Reverend Daniel Rogers, of Littleton, caused a disturbance in Newbury which added to the unrest in that town. The Reverend Nathaniel, of Ipswich, and his brother Daniel, who was seeking a pulpit, together with a third young candidate, gathered a crowd of people and traveled from Ipswich to Newbury. They entered the pulpit of the Reverend John Lowell in Newburyport without Mr. Lowell's consent, or the permission of the townsmen, the church, or the congregation. They presumably conducted a religious service in Mr. Lowell's pulpit, giving Daniel experience before an audience and perhaps showing the audience how dramatic New Light preaching was.

Then they moved to the First Parish in Newbury and tried to repeat the scene, but the Reverend Christopher Toppan was in the meetinghouse there, and managed to repulse the intruders. The disturbance probably unnerved Mr. Toppan, for it was said he began to carry a whip into the meetinghouse under his cloak in case he would need to "scorge out the enthusiasts" or "schemers," as he called them.

It was the Reverend Daniel Rogers, of Littleton, the cousin of these enthusiasts, who was coming to Bedford to moderate a church meeting called to depose the Reverend Nicholas Bowes and open the pulpit to another minister. (*See* Joshua Coffin, A *Sketch of the History of Newbury, Newburyport, and West Newbury*, p. 164, *passim.*

36. Bedford town records, 8/22/1754.

37. Asa Burr, *Diary about French and Indian War of 1758; Accounts 1758–1771*, manuscript. Also, extracts from the diary and notebook of Captain William Bacon, published in a pamphlet, printed in 1901 for the dedication of a monument in the town of Walpole, Mass.

38. *Proceedings of the American Antiquarian Society*, LXXVI, 197.

39. Harriette Merrifield Forbes, *Gravestones of Early New England and the Men Who Made Them*, pp. 81–84.

III. *Reverend Mr. Nathaniel Sherman*

1. Miller (*Errands, op. cit.*, p. 155) says Edwards was dismissed from Northampton and moved to Stockbridge where he was a missionary to a village of Indians. He was, however, still the leader of the revival movement, and was invited to be the president of the College of New Jersey (Nassau Hall) after Burr's death, but he died shortly after he took office.

2. Gaustad (*op. cit.*) points out that there were three schools whose founding was directly related to the influence of the Great Awakening. Besides Princeton, there were Dartmouth College, 1754, founded by New Light Eleazer Wheelock, and Brown University, 1764, founded as a Baptist college by James Manning, a graduate of Princeton in 1762.

3. Mary's parents were Benjamin and Mary. Benjamin was the brother of Mehitabel (Wellington) Sherman. However, Mary Lane's birth date as computed from her tombstone differs by two years from that in Hudson, *op. cit.*, pp. 687, 728.

4. Bedford town records, 11/17/1755.

5. For information on the stonecutter, see Peter Benes, "John Wight: The Hieroglyph Carver of Londonderry," in *The Bulletin of the Society for the Preservation of New England Antiquities*, LXIV, 2 (Fall of 1973), p. 31 *passim*.

6. Six of the deacon's children were married. Five were living in Townsend, Danvers, Middleton, and Topsfield, Massachusetts. The Deacon had given his oldest son, Israel Jr., twenty-two and a half acres of land in the southwest corner of his farm eleven years previously, when he had married. Israel, his wife, and four children lived there in a house they probably built. The Deacon's second son, Benjamin, and his youngest daughter, Bridget, were at home with the widow, Sarah (Bacon) Putnam.

The widow's third was set aside for Sarah. She had the lower east room and the bedroom adjoining on the back; the east garret and one third of the cellar on the south side; sufficient yard room before the house; the use of the oven in the other part of the house; the use of the well; twelve feet on the south side of the barn; the use of the barn floor for thrashing and bringing in hay; three-quarters of an acre of orchard; four and a half acres of tillage; three and three-quarters acres of meadow; a little more than six acres of woodland; one and one-half acres in Great Meadow; a little more than an acre in Elm Brook Meadow; and one third of a pew in Bedford meetinghouse.

All of the Deacon's children owned the remainder of the estate. Israel Jr. and Benjamin paid their brothers and sisters in cash for their shares and became tenants in common of the property. (Probate records, paper #18284; Registry of Deeds; statistics of Townsend; and Brown, *op. cit.*)

7. Gillies, *op. cit.*, p. 467.

8. Reverend Samuel Sewall, *History of Woburn*, p. 356.

9. Bedford town records, 12/12/1766.

10. Roger Sherman was a leading citizen in New Haven, Connecticut. He was a pillar of the White Haven Church during the ministry of Jonathan Edwards, Jr. (C. C. Goen, *Revivalism and Separatism*, pp. 190–91).

11. Henry R. Stiles, *History and Genealogies of Ancient Windsor*, I, 681–82; II.

IV. *Reverend Mr. Joseph Penniman*

1. Shattuck, *op. cit.*, p. 266.

2. *Ibid.*, p. 267.

3. Benjamin Kendall Emerson, *The Emerson Family*. Archibald MacLeish commemorated the founding of Conway, Mass., on its 200th anniversary, 1967, by writing a historical play about the town, which was adapted for television with the title: "An Evening's Journey to Conway, Massachusetts." It was given over Channel 2, WGBH-TV. The Reverend John Emerson was portrayed in it.

4. Joseph Willard, *A Sermon delivered* May 13, 1790, at the funeral of the Reverend Timothy Hilliard.

5. Samuel A. Bates, Ed., Records of the Town of Braintree, p. 421.

6. Morison, *op. cit.*, p. 95.

7. All but two of the men who preached in Bedford's pulpit were graduates of Harvard College between 1761 and 1767:

Abbott, Thomas (1764), dismissed from West Roxbury, tenets unknown

Bigelow, Jacob (1766), Arminian

Coogin, Jacob (1763), teacher in Bedford, tenets unknown

Dunbar, Asa (1767), dismissed from Salem, tenets unknown

Elliot, Andrew (1762), teacher at Harvard College, tenets unknown

Emerson, John (1764), Calvinist

Hilliard, Timothy (1764), would not speak on doubtful subjects

Hunt, Samuel (1765), tenets unknown

Johnson, Daniel (1767), tenets unknown

Moore, Jonathan (1761), dismissed for liberal views (from Rochester)

Sawyer, Amos, died

Thacher, Isaac, New Light Calvinist from Nassau Hall, New Jersey

Ward, Ephraim (1763), did not support ecclesiastical parties

Willard, Joseph (1765), Universalist.

8. Gillies, *Whitefield*, p. 221.

9. Bedford town records, 4/24/1771; Gillies, *op. cit.*, 470.
10. Service men directly related to families associated with the Bedford church, compiled from Brown, *op. cit.*, pp. 65–66:

Abbott, Moses, 48, son of the first covenantor, Obed
Bacon, Abijah, 25, Deacon Benjamin's nephew
Bacon, Elijah, 21, Deacon Benjamin's son
Bacon, Reuben, 17, Abijah's brother
Bacon, Samuel, 25, grandson of the first pew owner, Joseph
Davis, Eleazer, 41, son of the first covenantor, Eleazer
Davis, Josiah, 38, grandson of the first covenantor, Daniel
Davis, Samuel, 25, Josiah's brother
Davis, Thaddeus, 21, Deacon Stephen's son
Fassett, Asa, age unknown, son of the first covenantor, Josiah
Fitch, David, 32, son of the millowner, Benjamin
Fitch, Ebenezer, 24, nephew of Joseph, the meetinghouse builder
Fitch, Jeremiah, Jr., 33, the innkeeper's son
Fitch, John, 30, Jeremiah, Jr.'s brother
Fitch, Matthew, 30, John's twin brother
Fitch, Moses, 20, brother of Jeremiah, Jr., John, and Matthew
Gleason, Jonas, age not known, to buy a pew later
Hartwell, John, 20, grandson of the first covenantor, William, and son of Joseph
Hartwell, Joseph, 45, grandson of the first covenantor, William, and son of William; or 52, son of the first covenantor, William, and John's father
Hartwell, Samuel, 19, grandson of the first covenantor, William, and son of William
Hutchinson, Benjamin, about 52, son-in-law of the first pew owner, James Lane, and Martha (Minot) Lane
Jones, Timothy, age not known, to become a pew owner
Lane, David, 16, fifer, son of James and Mary (Wellington) Lane
Lane, James 3rd, 21, David's brother
Lane, Job, 58, Deacon Job's son
Lane, Job, Jr., 19, Deacon Job's grandson
Lane, John, 53, son of the first covenantor, John
Lane, John, Jr., 29, grandson of the first covenantor, John
Lane, Samuel, Jr., 38, John's brother
Lane, Samuel, 38, son of the first pew owner, James, and Martha (Minot) Lane
Lane, Solomon, 29, David's brother
Lane, Stephen, 20, Timothy's son
Lane, Timothy, 53, Deacon Job's son
*Maxwell, William, age not known, son of Hugh, who signed the church covenant under the administration of the Rev. Mr. Sherman

Merriam, John, 40, Deacon Nathaniel's grandson
Merriam, William, 25, John's brother
Moore, John, 46, who had a pew in the meetinghouse
Page, Christopher, 32, son of Christopher and grandson of the first covenantor, Nathaniel, and Susanna (Lane) Page
Page, David, 35, son of Nathaniel, Jr.
Page, Ebenezer, 38, son of John and grandson of the first covenantor, Nathaniel
Page, Nathaniel, Jr., 73, son of the first covenantor, Nathaniel
Page, Thomas, 42, son of Nathaniel, Jr.
Page, Timothy, 34, Ebenezer's brother
Page William, 37, son of Nathaniel, Jr.
Reed, David, age not known, relationship to John not known, to become a tavernkeeper
Reed, John, 44, owner of the Bowes's estate; or 17, the owner's son
Reed, Oliver, 45, brother of John, the owner of the Bowes's estate
Reed, Oliver, Jr., 20, nephew of the owner of the Bowes's estate
Putnam, Israel, 52, Deacon Israel's son
Putnam, Israel, Jr., 20, Deacon Israel's grandson
Stearns, Edward, 49, brother of the Rev. Mr. Josiah Stearns
Stearns, Solomon, 18, Edward's son
Webber, John, 43, husband of Sarah (Fassett) Webber who was Joseph Fassett's daughter
Wilson, Jonathan, 40, Thompson Bacon's stepfather
Wright, James, 30, later to be Deacon James Wright

11. Penniman's prayers and stories of his eccentricities are to be found in Brown, *op. cit.*; Shattuck, *op. cit.*; Nourse, *History of Harvard, Mass.*; and Brown, *Beneath Old Rooftrees*.

12. J. W. Thornton, *The Pulpit of the American Revolution*, p. 328.

13. See Note 11.

14. Bedford town records, 9/1/1783.

15. Brown, *Bedford, op. cit.*, p. 54.

16. Bedford town records, 3/4/1793.

17. See Note 11.

18. Brown, *Bedford, op. cit.*, p. 14.

19. *Ibid.*, and Ruth R. Wheeler, Concord, *Climate for Freedom*, pp. 69–70; Mrs. Wheeler says the Reverend John Whiting of Concord had this trouble. He would have a hangover on Sunday morning, and be unable to preach. The town would hire Timothy Minot as a substitute,

---

* William's brother, Thompson Maxwell, had been at the Boston Tea Party. Thompson lived in Milford, New Hampshire, and drove loads of supplies to Boston. He stopped in Bedford to visit Jonathan Wilson on his way through. Jonathan's first wife had been Thompson's sister. He went with Jonathan to the battle in Concord.

and trouble arose because the town was paying twice for the public worship service.

20. Bedford town records, 9/16/1793.

21. Information on the members of the council came from many sources: Weis, *Colonial Clergy*; Sprague, *Annals of the American Pulpit*; Malone, *Dictionary of American Biography*; histories of their towns; and sermons where available.

22. Sprague, *op. cit.*, VIII, 55–57.

23. Jacob Cushing, *A Sermon* at the ordination of Reverend Jacob Bigelow.

24. Brown, *Bedford*, p. 14.

25. According to Miss Elmira Scrooby, historian of Harvard, who has personal knowledge of the site of the old Davis farm and an understanding of the religious history of the town.

26. See Note 11.

27. *Ibid.*

28. *Ibid.*

V. *The Reverend Mr. Samuel Stearns*

1. The only source of the life of Samuel Stearns appears to be the biography written by his son, William Augustus Stearns. Much of the material in this section was taken from this source, especially the story of the conflict in Samuel's later life.

2. G.M. (The Reverend George Mooar), *The Historical Manual of the South Church in Andover, Mass.*, p. 105.

3. *Congregational Quarterly*. Boston: The American Congregational Association.

4. *Ibid.*, (April 1868), pp. 185–86.
shared the pulpit in Ipswich as colleaues; his cousin John was preaching
counts 1758–1771, manuscript. Also, extracts from the diary and note-

5. See Byington, *The Puritan, op. cit.*, p. 164, where reference is made to earlier sources.

6. The ring has been found in recent excavations at the site of John Hancock's first home, and is on display in the Lexington Historical Society's museum.

7. The story of the tragedy is printed at the end of a sermon delivered at Bedford, 7/1/1810, being the Sabbath after the death of Mr. Bacon, "who was shot through the body, June 2, by Mr. William Merriam."

8. *Congregational Quarterly, op. cit.* (July 1868), pp. 246–48.

9. Bedford town records, 4/1/1815.

10. Sidney Perley, *Historic Storms of New England*, Chapter 52.

11. Bedford town records, 12/11/1815.

12. Asher Benjamin (edited by Aymar Emsbury II), pp. 2, 39; also, Benjamin's *A New System of Architecture*, p. 87 (plate 38); 89 (plate

39). (The author is indebted to Roland Shaine of Lexington, Massachusetts, for the gift of this material.)

13. Brown, *Bedford*, pp. 54–55.

14. Bedford town records, 5/1/1817.

15. *Ibid.*, 6/26/1817.

16. *Ibid.*, 4/3 and 4/25/1824; 4/18 and 4/27/1829.

17. Stowe, *Saints, Sinners and Beechers*, p. 44.

18. Beecher, *Autobiography*, II, 73, 87; L. R. Paige, *History of Cambridge*, p. 557 and supplement. (Dr. Chaplin married in 1807 and was buried 10/14/1828.)

19. Bedford town records, 11/14/1831.

20. *Ibid.*

21. *Congregational Quarterly* (July 1868), p. 254.

22. *Ibid.*, p. 255.

23. William Augustus Stearns mentions 23 persons being admitted, but gives no names. The following list is extracted from a list of members of the Congregational Society in Bedford, 1843, which includes dates of admittance, and is on file at the Unitarian Historical Library in Boston. Those admitted on December 11, 1831, were:

Bacon, Isaac Preston, great-grandson of Deacon Benjamin and Catherine (Lane) Bacon, later to be named deacon of the Trinitarian Church

Clark, Mrs. Caroline G., wife of Daniel who is unknown

Colburn, Joseph, unknown

Davis, Eleazer Page, great-great-grandson of the first covenantor, Eleazer

Davis, Thaddeus H., great-great-grandson of the first covenantor, Stephen, later to be named deacon of the Trinitarian Church

Everett, William, a resident of about ten years

Gleason, Mrs. Lucy, née Butler; second wife of Louis Putnam Gleason, who moved to Bedford from Connecticut in 1821

Hartwell, Joseph, grandson of the first covenantor, William; or great-grandson of William and brother of Mary Joanna

Hartwell, Mary Joanna, great-granddaughter of the first covenantor, William

Hosmer, Leander, son of John, who had moved from Lexington to Bedford by way of Shrewsbury about 1790

Johnson, Mrs. Abigail M., wife of Obediah, below

Johnson, Obediah, moved to Bedford from Rindge, New Hampshire lately

Lane, Mrs. Betsey, née Simonds, wife of David, Jr., great-grandson of James and Martha (Minot) Lane

Munroe, Mrs. Mary Ann, née Stearns, daughter of Abner; second wife of Jonas whose first wife had been Abigail Stearns, daughter of the minister

Stearns, Franklin, unknown

Stearns, Mrs. Sally, née Cole, wife of Simeon, the minister's cousin
Webber, Mrs. Mary Ann, née Twist, wife of Benjamin
White, Widow Dorcas, unknown

24. Beecher, *Autobiography*, II, 371.
25. *Congregational Quarterly* (July 1868), p. 258.
26. *Ibid.* (October 1868), p. 367.
27. *Ibid.* (July 1868), p. 258; Bedford town records, 3/5/1832.
28. *Congregational Quarterly* (October 1868), p. 363.
29. *Ibid.* (July 1868), p. 260.
30. Samuel A. Eliot, *Heralds of a Liberal Faith*, II, 164–67.
31. Bedford town records, 2/27/1833.
32. *Congregational Quarterly* (July 1868), p. 271.
33. Bedford town records, 4/22/1833.
34. Alvan Lamson, *First Church and Parish in Dedham* "Sermon III," Herman Mann, Dedham, 1839, p. 70 (note o); pp. 98–99; and for an informal discussion, *see* Roy Johnson in the Boston *Globe*, 1/30/1966.
35. *Congregational Quarterly* (October 1868), p. 366.
36. *Ibid.*, p. 372.
37. *Ibid.*, p. 374. The church selected Jonathan Leavitt to fill its vacant pulpit. Mr. Leavitt was the husband of Charlotte Esther, daughter of Samuel and Abigail Stearns.

Notes on the Illustrations

Fig. 2. From Will Everett Eaton, *op. cit.*, p. 235. *See* Bibliography.
Fig. 3. Drawn from an old painting by Amos Doolittle, 1775, in the Concord Antiquarian Society Collection.
Fig. 4. From Levi S. Gould, *op. cit.*, p. 282. *See* Bibliography.
Fig. 5. Frontispiece from Abram English Brown, *History of Bedford, op. cit. See* Bibliography.
Fig. 6. Nicholas Bowes's ink stand is made of Colonial brass, and is in the Concord Antiquarian Society Collection.
Fig. 12. As described by the Reverend Henry A. Hazen, *op. cit.*, pp. 175–76. *See* Bibliography.
Fig. 17. From Joshus Coffin, *op. cit. See* Bibliography.
Fig. 18. From John Gillies, *op. cit. See* Bibliography.
Fig. 35. From Abram English Brown, *op. cit. See* Bibliography.
Fig. 39. *Ibid.*, Genealogical Section, p. 36.

BIBLIOGRAPHY

BIBLIOGRAPHY

Adams, James Truslow. *New England in the Republic, 1776–1850.* Boston: Little, Brown and Co., 1926.

Adams, Moses. *Sermon at the Death of Rev. Josiah Bridge.* (Pamphlet) Boston: Manning and Loring, 1801.

Bacley, Sarah Loring. *Historical Sketches of Andover, Mass.* Boston: Houghton Mifflin Co., 1880.

Bacon, Captain William. "Diary," published in *The Dedication to the Memory of the Men of Walpole and Vicinity who served in the French and Indian Wars.* (Pamphlet) Worcester: The American Antiquarian Society.

Baldwin, Thomas William. *Michael Bacon of Dedham, 1640, and His Descendants.* Cambridge (Mass.): Murry and Emery Co., 1915.

Barber, John Warner. *The History and Antiquities of New England, New York, New Jersey, and Pennsylvania.* Portland (Maine): William C. Lord, 1848.

Barnard, Thomas. *Sermon at the Interment of Rev. Phillips Payson.* (Pamphlet) Charlestown: Samuel Etheridge, 1801.

Bates, Samuel A., Ed. *Records of the Town of Braintree, Mass.* Randolph, Mass.: Daniel Huxford, 1886.

Bedford Town Records.

Beecher, Charles. *Autobiography and Correspondence of Lyman Beecher.* New York: Harper and Brothers, 1864.

Beers, F. W. *County Atlas of Middlesex.* New York: J. B. Beers and Co., 1875.

Benjamin Asher. *A New System of Architecture.* New York: Dover Reprint, 1969.

Bogart, Ernest L. and Kemmerer, Donald L. *Economic History of the American People.* New York: Longmans Green and Co., 1947.

Bond, Henry. *History of Watertown.* Boston: Little, Brown Co., 1855.

Bradford, Alden. *History of Massachusetts.* Boston: Wells and Lilly, 1825.

Bridge, Josiah and Adams, Moses. *Sermon at the Ordination of Luther Wright, and the Charge.* (Pamphlet) Dedham (Mass.): Mann and and Adams, 1798.

Brown, Abram English. *Beneath Old Rooftrees.* Boston: Lee and Shepard, 1896.

———. *History of the Town of Bedford.* Bedford (Mass.) Privately printed, 1891.

Brown, John. *The Pilgrim Fathers of New England and their Puritan Successors.* Boston: Fleming H. Revell Co., 1895.

Bryant, William Cullen and Gay, Sydney Howard. *A Popular History of the United States.* New York: Charles Scribner's Sons, 1881.

Bulkeley, Peter. *The Gospel Covenant or the Covenant of Grace Opened.* London: Benjamin Allen, 1646.

———. *Letter to Cotton Mather.* (Original) Worcester: The American Antiquarian Society.

Burr, Asa. *Diary of Asa Burr of Bellingham, Mass.* (Manuscript) Worcester: American Antiquarian Society.

Bushman, Richard L. *From Puritan to Yankee, Character and Social Order in Connecticut.* Cambridge (Mass.): Harvard University Press, 1967.

Byington, Ezra Hoyt. *The Puritan in England and New England.* Boston: Little, Brown and Co., 1900.

Chandler, Rev. Seth. *History of Shirley, Mass.* Privately printed, 1883.

Cherry, Conrad. *The Theoloy of Jonathan Edwards: A Reappraisal.* New York: Doubleday and Co., 1966.

Clark, George L. *A History of Connecticut.* New York: G. P. Putnam's Sons, 1914.

Cleveland, Mrs. Mary. *Diary of Mary Cleveland.* (Manuscript). Salem, (Mass.): Essex Institute.

Coffin, Joshua. *A Sketch of the History of Newbury, Newburyport, and West Newbury.* Boston: Samuel G. Drake, 1845.

Cole, Nathan. Diary (Facsimile). Hartford: The Connecticut Historical Society.

Concord Town Records and Vital Statistics.

"Confession of Faith and Form of the Covenant." (Bulletin) Boston: Unitarian Historical Library. Crocker & Brewster, 1821.

Congregational Quarterly. Boston: The American Congregational Association.

Cook, Frederick W. *Historical Data Relating to the Counties, Cities, and Towns in Mass.* Printed by the State at intervals.

Cushing, Jacob. *A Sermon at the Ordination of Reverend Jacob Bigelow.* (Pamphlet) Boston: T. and J. Fleet, 1772.

———. *Christian Ministers Commissioned by the Great Head of the Church to Preach the Gospel. (Listed in a sermon preached Nov. 21, 1792, at the ordination of Mr. Nathan Underwood).* Pamphlet. Boston: Thomas and John Fleet, 1793.

Davis, Rev. Emerson. *Biographical Sketches of Congregational Pastors of New England.* Boston: Unitarian Historical Library. Publisher unknown.

Drake, Samuel. *History of Middlesex County.* Boston: Estes and Lauriat, 1880.

Durant, Will and Ariel. *Rousseau and Revolution.* New York: Simon and Schuster, 1967.

Dwight, N. *The Lives of the Signers of the Declaration of Independence.* Cincinnati: A. S. Barnes and Co., 1851.

Eaton, Will Everett. *Proceedings of the 250th Anniversary of the Ancient Town of Reading.* Reading (Mass.): Loring and Twombly, 1896.

Eliot, Samuel A. *Heralds of a Liberal Faith.* Boston: American Unitarian Assn., 1910.

Ellis, Arthur B. *History of the First Church in Boston 1630–1880.* Boston: Hall and Whitney, 1881.

Emerson, Benjamin Kendall. *The Emerson Family.* Boston: David Clapp and Son, 1900.

Emsbury, Aymer II, Ed. *Reprints of Asher Benjamin.* New York: The Architectural Book Publishing Co., 1917.

Forbes, Harriette Merrifield. *Gravestones of Early New England and The Men Who Made Them.* Boston: Houghton Mifflin Co., 1927.
————. *New England Diaries 1602–1800.* Topsfield (Mass.): The Perkins Press, 1923.

Freeman, Samuel. *The Town Officer.* Boston: Thomas and E. T. Andrews, 1793.

Gaustad, Edwin Scott. *The Great Awakening.* Gloucester, (Mass.): Peter Smith, 1965 (Reprint).

Gillies, John. *Memoirs of Reverend George Whitefield.* New Haven: Whitmore and Buckingham, 1834.

Goen, C. C. *Revivalism and Separation in New England 1740–1800.* Hamden, (Conn.): Archon Books, The Shoestring Press, 1969.

Gould, Levi S. *Ancient Middlesex.* Somerville (Mass.): *Somerville Journal* Print, 1905.

Grant, Charles S. *Democracy in the Frontier Town of Kent.* New York: W.W. Norton Co., Inc., 1972.

Greven, Phillip J., Jr., *Four Generations.* Ithaca: Cornell University Press, 1970.

Hamilton, Edward P. *The French and Indian Wars.* New York: Doubleday and Co., Inc., 1962.

Hartwell, John F. *The Hartwells of America.* Little Rock, (Ark.): Privately published, 1956.

Hazen, Rev. Henry A. *History of Billerica.* Boston: A. Williams and Co., 1883.

Heimert, Alan. *Religion and the American Mind from the Great Awakening to the Revolution.* Cambridge (Mass.): Harvard University Press, 1966.

Holmes, Abiel. *The Life of Ezra Stiles.* Boston: Thomas and Andrews, 1798.

Hudson, Alfred Sereno. *History of Sudbury, Mass.* Privately published, 1889.

Hudson, Charles. *History of Lexington* (revised by the Lexington Historical Society). Boston: Houghton Mifflin Co., 1913.

Jackson, Francis. *History of Newton.* Boston: Stacy and Richardson, 1854.

Johnson, Roy. Article in the *Boston Globe,* Jan. 30, 1966.

Kendal, Samuel. *A Sermon at the Ordination of Avery Williams.* (Pamphlet) Boston: Munroe, Francis, and Parker, 1808.

Lamson, Alvan. *A History of the First Church and Parish in Dedham.* Dedham (Mass.): Herman Mann, 1839.

Lewis, Alonzo and Newhall, James R. *History of Lynn.* Privately printed, 1865.

Lockridge, Kenneth A. *A New England Town: The First Hundred Years.* New York: W.W. Norton and Co., Inc., 1970.

Love, W. DeLoss, Jr. *The Fast and Thanksgiving Days of New England.* Boston: Houghton Mifflin Co., 1895.

McLoughlin, William G. (Oscar Handlin, Ed.) *Isaac Backus and the American Pietistic Tradition.* Boston: Little, Brown and Co., 1967.

Malone, Dumas. *Dictionary of American Biography.* New York: Charles Scribner's Sons, 1934.

Mansur, Ina. "The Common, an Inconclusive Question," Bedford (Mass.) *Minuteman,* Feb. 19, 1970.

————. *The Story of the First Parish in Bedford, Unitarian Universalist.* (Pamphlet) Printed for the First Parish, 1967.

Marrett, Reverend John. "Diary" in Brown, *Beneath Old Rooftrees, op. cit.*

Massachusetts Historical Society, *Proceedings of,* 1875–76.

Mather, Cotton. *Magnalia Christi, Americana.* Hartford: Silas Andrus, 1820.

Mead, Sidney E. *The Lively Experiment, the Shaping of Christianity in America.* New York: Harper and Row, 1963.

Miller, Perry. *Errand Into the Wilderness.* New York: Harper and Row, 1964.

————. *Jonathan Edwards,* The American Men of Letters Series. New York: William Sloan Associates, 1949.

————. *Orthodoxy in Massachusetts 1630–1650.* Boston: Beacon Press, 1959.

————. *The New England Mind from Colony to Province.* Boston: Beacon Press, 1961.

Minot, James Grafton. *A Genealogical Record of the Minot Family in America and England.* Boston: Privately printed, 1897.

G.M. (The Reverend George Mooar) *Historical Manual of the South Church in Andover, Mass.* Andover: Warren F. Draper, 1859.

Morgan, Edmund S. *The Gentle Puritan: A Life of Ezra Stiles.* New Haven: Yale University Press, 1962.

Morison, Samuel Eliot. *Three Centuries of Harvard 1636–1936.* Cambridge: Harvard University Press, 1936.

Morrison, Hugh. *Early American Architecture.* New York: Oxford University Press, 1952.

Morse, Jedidiah. *The American Universal Geography.* Boston: Richardson and Lord, 1819.

New England Historical and Genealogical Register.

Nourse, Henry S. *History of Harvard (Mass.).* Harvard: Warren Hapgood, 1894.

Paige, Lucius R. *History of Cambridge, Mass., 1630–1877.* Boston: H. O. Houghton and Co., 1877.

Palmer, Joseph. *Necrology of Alumni of Harvard College.* Boston: John Wilson and Sons, 1864.

Payson, Rev. Phillips. *Sermon at the Ordination of Oliver Everett.* (Pamphlet) Boston: Nathaniel Coverly and Robert Hodge, 1782.

———. *Sermon at the Ordination of Seth Payson.* (Pamphlet) Boston: T. and J. Fleet, 1783.

———. *Sermon at the Ordination of Samuel Payson.* (Pamphlet) Boston: Thomas and John Fleet, 1762.

———. *Sermon at the Ordination of John Payson.* (Pamphlet) Boston: Richard Draper, 1768.

———. *Sermon at the Death of George Washington.* (Pamphlet) Charlestown, (Mass.): Samuel Etheridge, 1800.

Perley, Sidney. *Historic Storms of New England.* Salem (Mass.): The Salem Press and Publishing Co., 1891.

Pope, Robert S. *The Half-Way Covenant, Church Membership in Puritan New England.* Princeton: Princeton University Press, 1969.

Putnam, Aaron. "Against Universalism," a sermon included in *A Treatise Wherein Are Contained Several Particular Subjects.* Hartford (Conn.): Hudson & Goodwin, 1804.

Registry of Deeds for Middlesex County, North. Lowell, Mass.

Registry of Deeds for Middlesex County, South. Cambridge, Mass.

Salem, Mass., Vital Statistics.

Sewall, Rev. Samuel. *History of Woburn.* Boston: Wiggins and Lunt, 1868.

Shattuck, Lemuel. *History of the Town of Concord.* Boston: Russell Odiorne and Co., 1835.

Shipton, Clifford K. *Sibley's Harvard Graduates.* Boston: Massachusetts Historical Society.

Sinnott, Edmund W. *Meetinghouse and Church in Early New England.* New York: McGraw Hill Book Co., 1963.

Slosser, Gaius Jackson, Ed. *They Seek a Country, the American Presbyterians.* New York: The MacMillan Co., 1955.

Stearns, Josiah. *Sermon* (preached at Epping, New Hampshire, 1777). Pamphlet. Boston: The Pilgrim Library.

Stearns, George A. *The First Parish in Waltham*. Privately printed, 1914.
Stearns, Rev. Samuel. *Sermon Delivered at Bedford, July 1, 1810, at the Death of David Bacon*. (Pamphlet) Andover (Mass.): Galen Ware, 1810.
―――. *Sermon at Dunstable at the Ordination of Ebenezer Sperry*. (Pamphlet) Amherst, (N.H.): R. Boylston, 1813.
―――. *Sermon at Foxboro at the Ordination of Thomas Skelton*. (Pamphlet) Charlestown (Mass.): Jonathan Howe, 1809.
―――. *Sermon at Milton at the Ordination of Samuel Gile*. (Pamphlet) Boston: Belcher and Armstrong, 1807.
―――. *Sermon at the North Church, Reading*. (Pamphlet) Salem (Mass.): John D. Cushing and Brothers, 1822.
―――. *Discourse Delivered at Bedford, July 8, 1817, at the Dedication of the Meetinghouse*. (Pamphlet) Concord (Mass.): J.T. Peters, 1817.
Stearns, William Augustus. *Biography of the Rev. Samuel Stearns. Congregational Quarterly* (Jan., April, July, and Oct), 1868.
Stiles, Henry R. *The History and Genealogies of Ancient Windsor, Connecticut*. Hartford: Case, Lockwood, and Brainard, 1891.
Stone, Micah. *A Christian People's Remembrance of their Deceased Pastor. A sermon preached at the death of Ephraim Ward*. (Pamphlet) Brookfield (Mass.): E. Merriam and Co., 1818.
Stowe, Lyman Beecher. *Saints, Sinners, and Beechers*. Indianapolis: Bobbs-Merrill Co., 1934.
Thatcher, Thomas. *A Sermon at the Ordination of Joseph Tuckerman, Boston, Masss., 1801*. (Pamphlet) Worcester: American Antiquarian Society.
Thornton, John Wingate. *The Pulpit of the American Revolution*. Boston: Gould Lincoln, 1860.
Vital Statistics of Harvard, Mass.
Walcott, Charles H. *Concord in the Colonial Period*. Boston: Estes and Lauriat, 1884.
Walker, Williston. *A History of the Congregational Churches in the United States*. New York: The Christian Literature Co., 1897.
Ware, Henry. *The Ware Family, Descendants of Henry Ware*. (1893 manuscript) Worcester: American Antiquarian Society.
Waters, Rev. Wilson. *History of Chelmsford, Massachsuetts*. Lowell: Courier Citizen, 1917.
Webster, Henry Sewall. *Silvester Gardiner*. Gardiner (Maine): Historical Series No. 2, 1913.
Weis, Frederick Lewis. *The Colonial Clergy and the Colonial Churches of New England*. Lancaster (Mass.), 1936.
Wertenbaker, Thomas Jefferson. *Princeton 1746–1896*. Princeton: Princeton University Press, 1946.
Wheeler, Ruth R. *Concord: Climate for Freedom*. Concord (Mass.): Concord Antiquarian Society, 1967.

White, Rev. Henry. *The Early History of New England.* Concord (N.H.): S. Boyd, 1841.

Willard, Joseph. *Willard Memoir.* Boston: Phillips, Sampson and Co., 1858.

Willard, Joseph and Walker, Charles W. *Willard Genealogy.* Boston: 1915.

Willard, Joseph. *Sermon Delivered at the Funeral of the Rev. Timothy Hilliard.* (Pamphlet) Boston: Samuel Hall, 1790.

Winslow, Ola Elizabeth. *Jonathan Edwards 1703–1758.* New York: The MacMillan Co., 1940.

———. *Meetinghouse Hill.* New York: The MacMillan Co., 1953.

Winthrop, John. (James Savage, Ed.) *The History of New England, 1630–1649.* Boston: Little Brown and Co., 1880.

Wish, Harvey, Ed. *The Diary of Samuel Sewall.* New York: G. P. Putnam's Sons, 1967.

Wright, Conrad. *The Beginnings of Unitarianism in America.* Boston: Beacon Press, 1955.

Zeichner, Oscar. *Connecticut's Years of Controversy 1750–1775.* Hamden: Archon Books, The Shoestring Press, 1970.

Zuckerman, Michael. *New England Towns in the Eighteenth Century.* New York: Alfred A. Knopf, 1970.

INDICES

INDEX OF PERSONS

232